C0-ALR-542

Praise for *Everyday Tarot Magic*

"By showing you how to combine imaginative visualizations and affirmations with accessories like candles, herbs, and crystals, Dorothy Morrison helps you activate the magic within the images of the Tarot. Her simple but dynamic rituals will bring vitality into your daily routine, and enable you to manifest your personal vision of a beautiful life."

—Janina Renée
Author of *Tarot Spells, Tarot for Every Day,*
and *Tarot for a New Generation*

"This wonderful book will delight anyone looking for an in-depth magical approach to Tarot, providing explanations of the cards and their use in readings, a superb spell section, guidelines for utilising Tarot for self-development, and much more. Dorothy Morrison's clear, reassuring style will give newcomers confidence, whilst the experienced will find plenty to expand their knowledge and enhance their practice."

—Elen Hawke
Author of *In The Circle, The Sacred Round,*
and *Praise to the Moon*

"*Everyday Tarot Magic* provides an interesting and detailed look into using the Tarot as a magical tool. Dorothy Morrison offers a complete and powerful guide for those who want to incorporate the cards into their magic on a daily basis."

—Yasmine Galenorn
Author of several books, including *Crafting the Body Divine*
and *Embracing the Moon*

Everyday

Tarot

magic

About the Author

Dorothy Morrison is a Wiccan High Priestess of the Georgian Tradition. She founded the Coven of the Crystal Garden in 1986. An avid practitioner of the Ancient Arts for more than twenty years, she spent many years teaching the Craft to students throughout the United States and Australia and is a member of the Pagan Poet's Society.

To Write to the Author

If you wish to contact the author or would like more information about this book, please write to the author in care of Llewellyn Worldwide and we will forward your request. Both the author and publisher appreciate hearing from you and learning of your enjoyment of this book and how it has helped you. Llewellyn Worldwide cannot guarantee that every letter written to the author can be answered, but all will be forwarded. Please write to:

Dorothy Morrison
℅ Llewellyn Worldwide
P.O. Box 64383, Dept. 0-7387-0175-0
St. Paul, MN 55164-0383, U.S.A.

Please enclose a self-addressed stamped envelope for reply, or $1.00 to cover costs. If outside U.S.A., enclose international postal reply coupon.

Many of Llewellyn's authors have websites with additional information and resources. For more information, please visit our website at http://www.llewellyn.com.

Everyday

Tarot

magic

MEDITATION & SPELLS

DOROTHY MORRISON

2003
Llewellyn Publications
St. Paul, Minnesota 55164-0383, U.S.A.

Everyday Tarot Magic © 2002 by Dorothy Morrison. All rights reserved. No part of this book may be used or reproduced in any manner whatsoever, including Internet usage, without written permission from Llewellyn Publications except in the case of brief quotations embodied in critical articles and reviews.

First Edition
Second Printing, 2003

Book design and editing by Karin Simoneau
Cover design by Kevin R. Brown
Cover images: *The Nigel Jackson Tarot* © 2000, illus. by Nigel Jackson

Library of Congress Cataloging-in-Publication Data
Morrison, Dorothy, 1955–
 Everyday tarot magic : meditation & spells / Dorothy Morrison.
  p. cm.
 Includes bibliographical references.
 ISBN 0-7387-0175-0
 1. Tarot. 2. Magic. I. Title
BF1879.T2 M685 2002
133.3'2424—dc21   2002030058

Llewellyn Worldwide does not participate in, endorse, or have any authority or responsibility concerning private business transactions between our authors and the public.

All mail addressed to the author is forwarded but the publisher cannot, unless specifically instructed by the author, give out an address or phone number.

Any Internet references contained in this work are current at publication time, but the publisher cannot guarantee that a specific location will continue to be maintained. Please refer to the publisher's website for links to authors' websites and other sources.

Llewellyn Publications
A Division of Llewellyn Worldwide, Ltd.
P.O. Box 64383, Dept. 0-7387-0175-0
St. Paul, MN 55164-0383, U.S.A.
www.llewellyn.com

 Printed on recycled paper in the United States of America

Also by Dorothy Morrison

Magical Needlework

Everyday Magic

In Praise of the Crone: A Celebration of Feminine Maturity

The Whimsical Tarot

Yule: A Celebration of Light & Warmth

Bud, Blossom, & Leaf:
The Magical Herb Gardener's Handbook

The Craft: A Witch's Book of Shadows

The Craft Companion

For Z. Harrell, whose love of the Tarot—and its magic—
is my constant source of inspiration.

In Memory of . . .

Scheryll "Lady Duvessa" Baxter, who passed from this world on August 5, 2002. Your many kindnesses, nurturing love, and unyielding support enriched more lives than you'll ever know. I miss you deeply.

Contents

Acknowledgments

Just as the Fool cannot complete his journey without interacting with others along the path, such is the case with a book. Wonderfully capable folks who edit and illustrate come into play. Those who print, publish, market, and publicize are important, too. But the assistance necessary to turn out a good book goes far beyond that. It takes people who encourage, who inspire, and even those who disagree so adamantly that they force the author to sit back and rethink the very concept of his or her message. Without them, there would be no path, no journey, no hope of attaining cyclic manifestation. And it's those people to whom I, the Fool and seeker, owe a huge vote of thanks; for each—in his or her own special way—has not only assisted me in completing a very personal journey, but played an important role in bringing this book from my hands to yours.

To Mark—my husband and the love of my life—whose capacity for patience and understanding is unsurpassed, and who lights my World every day with his gentle touch and captivating smile.

To my sister, Mary Anne—a High Priestess in her own right—whose ability to walk between the worlds consistently reminds me that everything is possible.

To Trish Telesco, the Empress, who nurtured, encouraged, and believed in me strongly enough to launch my flight toward a successful writing career.

To M. R. Sellars, the Emperor, whose loyalty as a friend and confidante is without measure, and whose sound advice keeps me ever striving toward perfection.

To A. J. Drew, the Hierophant and Prince of Yeti's, whose zest for life, ability to march to his own drummer, and devotion to those he loves makes me ever grateful for extended family, crossing paths, and divine intervention.

To Karri Ann Allrich, Barbara Ardinger, and Elen Hawke, who have been my Strength when I thought I couldn't go on, and my courage when they insisted I could.

To Nancy Mostad, the Chariot, whose knacks for friendship, gentle counsel, and sound advice have, in many ways, transformed me into the person I am today.

To Barbara Moore, the Star, who believed in this book enough to make it happen and brought my wish to reality.

To Karin Simoneau, my editor and the Sun, whose golden rays gild my words, warm my style, and shed a light on my message that I never thought possible.

To the Art, Publicity, Marketing, and Sales Departments, who, together, spin the Wheel of Fortune every day not only toward my ongoing success, but toward that of countless others in our growing community.

And to Carl, Sandra, and Gabe Weschcke, who, together in their role as the Magician, bring wonderful books to our community every day, that we may learn and grow as we embark upon the never-ending path of the personal spiritual journey.

Huge hugs, much love, and many thanks to you all!

Part One

Getting Started

The Tarot is a deck of cards
Once used by noble gents and lords
And ladies of the royal court
For parlor games of playful sort
But it's become now something more
A system that flings forth the door
To spiritual realms we cannot see
It traces steps we walk as we
Take on the business of this life
Revealing patterns wrought with strife
And patterns, too, of joyful glee
To form a perfect tapestry
But even still, it's something more
It brings advice toward what's in store
So we may change the current path
Escaping woeful aftermath
Of troubles that once blocked the way
And bringing us a brighter day

—Dorothy Morrison

1

The Tarot:
What It Is and Isn't

The history of the Tarot is speculative at best. In fact, no one—not even the most acclaimed Tarot scholars—seem to agree on its origins or historical value. One of the most popular theories is that the Tarot came to Europe by way of a nomadic group of Egyptians known as "Gypsies."[1] And even though there isn't sufficient evidence to support this notion, its supporters insist that the Tarot was not only based on an ancient book of personal development called *The Book of Thoth,* but that the mysteries of its wisdom were hidden within the illustrations of the Major Arcana.

A more widely accepted theory, however, is that the system originated in Italy, was born of a regular deck of playing cards, and began as nothing more than a parlor game designed to entertain early fifteenth-century Italian nobility. And though it's not nearly as romantic or appealing, this seems a bit more plausible. Why? For one thing, the earliest names attributed to the system, *carte da trionfi* and *tarrochi,* were Italian, and there was no recorded term in any other language to describe the deck for more than a century. For another, the original trump cards[2] did not depict Egyptian figures. Instead, they held illustrations of European court nobility. And that being the case, it only makes sense that the system originated in Europe rather than Egypt.

Perhaps more interesting than the actual origins of the Tarot, though, are the facts surrounding the playing cards it was born of. Designed by the Spanish Muslims in the early 1300s, these playing cards hit Europe sometime between 1375 and 1378. And though the decks did, indeed, incorporate four suits, the hearts, clubs, diamonds, and spades that we know today didn't exist until the French revised them in the late 1470s. Instead, the original suits were nearly identical to those we use in current Tarot decks: sticks or staves, swords, cups, and coins.

It's also interesting to note that the suit-related court cards—a king and two others that are lesser in value—were all masculine in nature. When the Tarot came into being, however, all that changed. A set of queens appeared, as did the Fool and the trump cards. It's important to understand that the additions had nothing to do with divination, though. They were simply necessary components for playing the original game—a game with trumps that was played much like bridge.

If that's the case, how did we come to use the Tarot as a spiritual device? How could a simple parlor game evolve into such an important tool? Since regular playing cards had been associated with fortunetelling since 1487, there's no reason to think that the Tarot escaped the seer's eye. However, it wasn't until some 350 years later that precise divinatory meanings were associated with the cards, and the illustrations were modified to reflect this. In fact, the Tarot wasn't even considered valuable to occult study until the early 1780s. It was at that point that the system took its place as an integral part of the philosophy and began its development into the powerful spiritual tool we know today.

How the Tarot Works

Regardless of its history, the Tarot is, without a doubt, one of the most useful spiritual tools at our disposal. That's because it not only bridges the gap between the mundane and spiritual worlds, but also delivers clear and accurate advice that we can use to our benefit. That's good news.

The best news, though, is that people can use it to empower their lives and increase their productivity. It doesn't take special card-reading skills or psychic ability. A high IQ isn't necessary, and neither is a red phone to the spirit world. All it takes is a firm desire, a little imagination, and the ability to follow a storyline. It's as simple as that.

Working with the Tarot comes easily because it speaks to us in images—a subliminal language that the brain not only understands, but uses to process every single thought we think. Here's how it works.

When we look at a picture, the mundane self (the conscious mind) immediately strikes up a conversation with the inner child (the subconscious mind). And as they talk, the subconscious mind searches the memory banks for every image that relates to that picture. The pictures form in the mind's eye and when that happens, both sectors of the spiritual self (the personal unconscious and the collective unconscious) come alive. The personal unconscious processes every bit of personal knowledge that we've ever accumulated in connection with that image. The collective unconscious gets busy, too—it searches out every related instinctual and intuitive reaction, draws its own conclusions, and matches those up with the data collected by the personal unconscious. Once they have all the information together, they tie it up into one nice, neat little package and deliver it to the conscious and subconscious minds. The brain's work is done and—voila!—we suddenly understand what the image is saying.

Even so, many people have difficulty using the Tarot. Why? Simply put, they just try too hard. They think that they're supposed to get some sort of mysterious set of messages. That being the case, they send their brains into overload with the search. And when it comes back empty-handed, they pack up the deck and put it aside, never to be used again.

The truth of the matter is that the Tarot is nothing more than a set of pictures designed to tell a story. In fact, it's much like reading a comic strip without the benefit of words. Once we determine what the characters are doing and how they're interacting, the message comes through loud and clear. There's nothing to ponder, nothing with which to tax our brains. We see it and understand it. End of story.

That's all well and fine. But other than the fact that the card images speak to all parts of the brain, what makes it a spiritual tool? Isn't it just another fortunetelling device?

Contrary to popular belief, the Tarot does not in any way forecast the future. Instead, it gives us choices and allows pause for thought. It taps into what we either cannot see or refuse to see on a mundane level, and puts it right in front of us. That, in itself, is quite a feat. But it doesn't stop there. It goes on to show us what is likely to happen if we continue upon the current path. We can then decide whether it's in our best interest to change the route or move forward as planned. And that's something a mere fortunetelling device can't do.

Finding the Right Deck

Long ago, my mother presented me with the Rider-Waite deck. I studied it. I worked with it. I even went as far as to memorize the instruction booklet. But no matter what I did, I simply couldn't make it work for me. To say that I was disgusted was the understatement of the century. I'd always been able to accomplish anything I'd put my mind to, and for the life of me, I just couldn't understand why I was having so much trouble. Suffice it to say, the deck finally wound up on a shelf—never to be used again—for even looking at it made me feel useless and stupid. As a result, I resolved never to pick up another Tarot deck again.

Of course, there was a lot I didn't understand about the Tarot back then. There was nothing wrong with the deck. There was nothing wrong with me. In fact, the only problem with either was that we just didn't belong together. Not knowing that, though, cost me dearly. And it almost kept me from ever discovering the empowering joys of the Tarot.

This doesn't have to happen to you. Finding the deck that's right for you isn't difficult, but shopping for it may take some patience. That's because there are literally hundreds of decks to choose from. And if it's your first deck, you may not even be sure of what you're looking for. It's a trial and error process much like finding the perfect outfit. You see it and like it, but can't get the whole picture until you try it on.

Fortunately, most stores that carry decks now have sample copies on hand. This allows you to look through the cards and play with them a bit before you buy. That's very important stuff, because there's nothing worse than taking something home that just won't work for you.

That being the case, be prepared to spend a little time—at least twenty minutes or so—with any deck that appeals to you. Examine each card and see how it makes you feel. Make a few notes. Pay special attention to the coloring, the imagery, and, of course, any emotional response that particular cards evoke in you. Then take your notepad and go home.

Leaving the store before you buy is imperative because it prevents the two most common problems involved when searching for a deck: first, you're not tempted to buy on impulse (impulsively purchased decks frequently wind up unused because they seldom really speak to you); and second, you're more apt to search a little further for the perfect deck if you haven't already purchased one.

With that in mind, wait a day or two and pull out your notes. Then take a good hard look at what you wrote down. Does the deck still appeal to you as much as it did then? Is the imagery still as vibrant within your mind's eye? If you can honestly answer "Yes!" to both questions, then it's definitely the deck for you. If not, keep searching. And above all, don't worry. The perfect deck will definitely present itself in short order!

One final note of advice—especially for beginners. It's much easier to work with a deck that provides full pictorial scenes on every card, rather than one that depicts only a set number of rods (also known as wands in many decks), cups, swords, or pentacles. In fact, after more than twenty years of experience with the Tarot, I still shy away from those. It's not that there's anything wrong with those decks per se, it's just that their images don't speak as loudly to the subconscious, and this makes it easy to miss the intended messages.

Blessing the Deck

Although using the Tarot isn't difficult, not many people would turn down an extra boost of energy to get the best performance possible. And I'm sure you're no exception. That's where blessing the deck comes in. It not only puts you in tune with the cards, but paves the road toward your own personal empowerment. It's something that's just too good to bypass.

I've provided a sample blessing ritual for you. Don't be afraid to vary from its guidelines or rework it to suit your lifestyle, though. Know that there is no right or wrong way to bless your deck, and that whatever you decide will work perfectly for you.

Materials
1 purple candle
Incense of your choice
Tarot deck
Water
Salt

Begin by lighting the candle and incense, and placing the deck in front of them. Close your eyes and inhale deeply through your nose. Exhale fully from your mouth. After four or five breaths, open your eyes and pass the deck through the incense smoke, saying something like:

> *I give you now the breath of Air*
> *Inhale its twirling riches, fair*

Being careful not to burn yourself or the cards, quickly pass the deck through the candle flame. Say something like:

I give you now the warmth of fire
So you may answer my desire

Lightly sprinkle the deck with a few drops of water, saying:

I give you water—life's true force
Drink deeply as you chart your course

Then sprinkle the deck with a few grains of salt, saying:

I give you earth that you may sow
The seeds of power, my Tarot

Finally, lift the deck skyward and say:

Power of the ancient Tarot
Bring your knowledge; let it flow
Into my soul—into my brain
From this deck, let knowledge rain

Then spend fifteen minutes or so in visualization mode. See yourself reading the cards with insight and accuracy, understanding every message completely.

Leave the deck in front of the candle until the wick burns out.

After the Blessing

The deck is blessed and it's ready for use, right? Well, that depends solely upon who you ask. Many folks subscribe to the "put the deck under your pillow and sleep with it" rule. Some disagree, saying that a new deck should be carted around in the purse or briefcase. Still others insist that the deck must be housed with an assortment of crystals—rose, smoky, and clear quartz, to be exact—wrapped in silk, and carried somewhere on the owner's body. The only thing they do agree upon is the length of the methodology: a one-week period.

You're not alone if you think these sound like strange preparation tactics. But the reasoning behind them is sound. Simply put, it's that constantly having the deck close to you for the first week literally saturates the cards with your personal energy. And that being the case, it stands to reason that the deck will always read well for you.

But I beg to differ. At one time or another, I tried each of the methods described above. The problem wasn't that they didn't work—the problem was that because my personal energy is quite strong, they simply worked too well. And as a result, no one else's energy was ever able to penetrate the cards—not even temporarily. No matter who shuffled the deck, the reading presented by the cards always seemed to reflect my energy and life, not the querent's.

For that reason, I urge you to try this first: spend some time—fifteen to twenty minutes—with your new deck every day for a week. Shuffle them. Look at them. Commit some of the images to memory. In short, bond with them. If, at a later date, you decide that you're not as well connected to your deck as you'd like to be, you can always try one of the other methods.

Storing the Deck

If you think disagreements fly fast and furious around deck preparation, you should hear the disputes regarding storage. I've heard everything you can imagine—from insulating the deck in silk to hiding it in a dark place where uninvited energy won't disturb it. There are also those who insist on specially prepared wooden storage boxes, velvet-lined pouches, and a plethora of other things. I could go on and on. Fact is, there are as many deck storage methods as there are folks who use the Tarot.

To be perfectly honest, I've never found that one particular storage method worked any better for me than another, or that any of them ever improved the performance of any deck I used. For that reason, I believe in keeping it simple. If you find a pouch, scarf, or box that appeals to you, so be it. But if you're just as comfortable keeping your cards together with a rubber band, that's okay, too. Just don't get caught up in an inner struggle over something as trivial as deck storage. Simply do whatever feels right to you, and know that you can't go wrong.

Getting to Know Your Cards

The Tarot is one of the most versatile spiritual tools available to us today. We can read it, then use its advice to solve our problems. We can employ it for self-discovery and personal empowerment. We can even use it to power our magic. Its knowledge is open to everyone, and all we have to do is reach out and grab it.

But before we can do any of that, we have to understand it. We have to get to know the cards. We have to know who they are, where they're coming from, and what individual purposes they hold. In fact, we have to allow them to become our most intimate friends. But how is that possible? They are, after all, just cards!

Not so fast, my friend. Each card depicts a character— or set of characters—with a personality, disposition, and temperament all its own. And knowing where that character is coming from makes all the difference in the world when it comes to understanding the message of its specific card. The best way to accomplish this is to follow the visualization/meditation exercise outlined below.

Card Meditation

Start by picking a card from the deck. (Although I usually suggest starting with the Major Arcana, any card will do as long as it appeals to you.) Now, study the imagery very carefully. Check out facial expression, body language, and character activity. Note how the card colors make you feel. Memorize the image and close your eyes. Visualize the card growing larger and larger until it fills the whole room. Then allow it to take on a three-dimensional form. This is important. Why? Because if the card depiction—characters, surroundings, and so forth—doesn't appear as real to you as the chair you're sitting on, you won't be able to get the full impact of this exercise.

Once you've gotten the image firmly fixed in your mind's eye, visualize yourself stepping into the card. (Depending upon card enlargement size, you may have to visualize yourself shrinking a bit to enter.) Take a few moments to acclimate yourself to the setting. Look at your surroundings. Study the atmosphere. Think about how being there makes you feel. Are you happy, sad, or indifferent? Are you calm and serene, or slightly agitated? It could be that you are none of the above, and that's okay, too. Whatever your feelings, though, make a mental note to remember them. You'll want to write them down when you've finished with the visit.

Now look at the characters in the card. See how they've come to life. Pay close attention to what they're doing, and how they're spending their time. Also take note of their body language, how they move, and—if there is more than one character in the card—how they interact with each other.

Once you've assessed the characters and their surroundings, step right up and introduce yourself. Say why you're there, and what you hope to gain by the visit. Remember to be pleasant and polite. (Even though these folks are not of this world, the idea here is to befriend them—and you won't be able to do that unless you're on your best behavior.) Ask direct questions, and listen carefully to the answers. See where the conversation goes. Then, when the discussion wanes, tell the characters how nice it was to have met them, and thank them for their time. Say goodbye and step out of the card. Make notes for future use.

While stepping into cards is fun and enlightening, there may come a time when a particular character or environment makes you feel uncomfortable. Should this happen, there's no need for alarm. Just step back out, and put the card aside. It only means that you're not quite ready for the full message of that card. You'll know when the time is right, and when it is, you can try that card again.

Just one more thing about the meditations. There's no need to do all seventy-eight at once. And it's certainly not necessary to complete them all before you begin to use the deck. Just do a few at a time. Work at your own pace. And, of course, enjoy the process. You are, after all, making new friends.

The Personal Tarot Guide

No matter how you choose to use the cards, help is the one thing you can always count on. It's not the sort you'll find from taking a class. You won't find it by reading a book. It won't even come from hours of serious study. The sort of help I'm talking about is a completely different type. It's an easy, free-flowing series of communications that comes directly from your personal Tarot guide.

This entity is much like the spirit guide, and everybody has one. It whispers in your ear, directs your thought processes, and puts you on the right track. And—if you're as stubborn as I am—it occasionally smacks you around with a Cosmic two-by-four when you don't pay attention. It's a wonderful spirit that's always ready to help with Tarot-related questions, answers, and solutions. All you have to do is ask.

While contacting the personal guide isn't difficult, it will take a few minutes of your time and some complete and undivided attention. For that reason, it's a good idea to clear the way of any possible interruptions. Turn off the ringer on your phone, and lower the volume on your answering machine. Then grab a small stone that appeals to you—fluorite, amethyst, clear quartz, and sodalite are all good choices and can be found at your local metaphysical shop—and quickly retreat to the most comfortable spot in your home. The key here is relaxation, so if sitting in your favorite chair, lying down on your bed, or even simmering in your bathtub will put you in that mode, that's the way to go.

Once you're comfortable, hold the stone in your dominant hand. Let go of any tensions and clear your mind. Then take a trip in your mind's eye. Go to someplace peaceful and serene. This could be a meadow, a beach, or a mountaintop. It might even be a room in a home you've visited before. The place, itself, isn't important. It's only important that it be a spot where you feel calm and happy.

Spend a few moments settling in and acclimating yourself to the surroundings. Then call your Tarot guide by saying something like:

> *Tarot guide, come forth to me*
> *I conjure you from depth of sea*
> *From fertile earth, from mountain breeze*
> *From dancing flame that warms with ease*
> *I call you, wisest Tarot guide*
> *To be forever at my side*
> *Make your presence known to me*
> *As I will, so mote it be*

Wait patiently, and your guide will appear.

It's important to note that guides are otherworldly creatures, so yours may not appear as human. It could take the form of an animal, a plant, or some other natural substance. It could also appear as a shadow, a twirling ball of color, or even a beacon of light. That's okay. Every guide looks different. Just know that whatever you see first is the shape and form that yours has chosen.

Once your guide appears, strike up a conversation. Tell it that you have embarked upon the journey of the Tarot and have summoned it for help. Then add a dose of flattery. (Tarot guides love that sort of thing.) Say that you not only want its help, but *need* it—that there's no way you can wade through the system without its power and wisdom. Then tell it how wonderful it is for coming to your aid, and how much you appreciate all its efforts.

Now sit quietly. Listen carefully to the responses. Pay close attention to everything it says. It may give you tips for working with the cards, or ideas for simplifying your personal journey. Everything your guide says is important, and you'll want to write it down later.

When the conversation wanes, tell your guide that you want to return its kindness. And that being the case, you're prepared to give it a real home—a place it can call its own. Explain that you will house it within the stone and keep it with your cards. That way, it will always be with you and the Tarot that it loves so much.

Listen for the response, then say goodbye.

The Tarot Guide Home Ritual

It's always a good idea to keep your promises, but this is especially true of those made to your Tarot guide. Otherwise, you can't expect it to help you—and help was the reason for contacting your guide in the first place. So follow through on your end of the deal. Give your guide a home. It won't take long and any effort will be well worth the results.

Materials

Incense of your choice (nagchampa, sandalwood, or frankincense work well here)

1 white or purple candle

Vanilla, rose, or rosewood oil

The stone used in the contact meditation

Your Tarot deck and storage device

Light the incense and anoint the candle with oil. Think about the relationship you've just formed with your Tarot guide. Concentrate on building the relationship into a real friendship, and everything that it entails. Then light the candle, saying:

> *I welcome you into my heart*
> *Come be my friend and never part*
> *Come share your secret thoughts and whims*
> *And I shall treasure them as gems*

Hold the stone to your third eye (the spot between your eyebrows) and say:

> *I promised I'd provide a space*
> *For you, alone—a peaceful place—*
> *A place where you could breathe and live*
> *And that is now just what I give*
> *Come and dwell within this stone*
> *The place that you can now call home*
> *Kept with cards, so safe and sound*
> *Where love and knowledge here abound*

Kiss the stone, place it on top of the deck, and leave it there until the candlewick burns out. Then store the stone and deck together.

Each time you work with the cards, call your guide from the stone by saying something like:

> *I call you forth, my Tarot guide*
> *In love and joy, stay at my side*

Reading Cards the Easy Way

Although there are many ways to use the Tarot, most folks really want to read it. They usually shy away from reading, however, for one of three reasons: (a) they think they have to memorize the card meanings; (b) they think they need an exorbitant amount of psychic ability for accuracy; or (c) they've heard that reading cards will leave them completely wiped out and exhausted. While we already know that memorization and psychic ability aren't necessary, card reading can drain the personal energy supply. This method, however, takes care of that problem, too. In fact, I often have more energy when I'm done than I did at the onset.

Just start by calling your Tarot guide and shuffling the deck. (Don't formulate a question; just keep your mind clear.) Turn up the first three cards, and view them as if they were a comic strip with no words. What are the characters doing? How are they interacting with each other? Are they facing each other or are their backs turned away? What do they have in common? More important, what story does this card combination tell? Just answer the questions and you'll be well on your way to quick, accurate, and tireless reading.

Still at a loss? Then let's say, for example, that the Ten of Cups, the Lovers, and the Ace of Pentacles come up, in that order. From this we can surmise that whichever partner is closest to the Ten of Cups sees the relationship as the love of a lifetime. In fact, this person is so madly in love that he or she is considering a long-term commitment. The other partner, however, views the relationship very differently, and is much more concerned with the steady source of income that will come from the union. Regardless of this person's nurturing actions or loving declarations, he or she has absolutely no intention of putting his or her heart on the line in any way, shape, or form. It isn't a good scenario.

However, if the cards in question were the King of Pentacles and the Queen of Cups, with the Ten of Cups falling in the center, the story would be much happier. This would say that both parties are interested in a loving, long-term commitment. Even better, this King is financially comfortable and doesn't mind seeing to it that his mate is as well. The Queen, on the other hand, is perfectly happy to offer the tender loving care that this King craves. It's a good match all the way around, and both parties can expect much happiness.

One more thing about reading the cards: while it's always a good idea to study the cards thoroughly, never discount your first reaction. The reason for this is that messages—even those you may consider to be nothing more than fleeting thoughts—often creep forth from the psyche. And listening to those can make all the difference in the world between an accurate reading and one that's only mediocre.

Reversals versus Uprights

Many good readers insist upon reading card reversals when they pop up. They feel that there's just no way to get the full picture unless these meanings are incorporated. And since this reasoning is based in logic, it certainly seems sound. This is one point, however, on which I beg to differ. Here's why:

Many years ago, I embarked upon a thorough exploration of Tarot spreads that involved some heavy experimentation with upright and reversed cards. First, I read the cards just as they came up, reversals and all. Then I turned the reversals upright, and read the spreads again. What I found was amazing. The readings were identical, and the resulting advice was the same.

Of course I'm the practical sort, so I thought it was a fluke. And so I tried again . . . and again . . . and again. In fact, I was so entranced by the phenomenon that my experiment continued for a good six months and included many other readers. Never once did the results vary. They were always the same.

All at a loss, we sat down to think. And finally, it hit us: like life, the Tarot is a system of checks and balances. For every positive card, there is a negative. And that being the case, the readings simply balanced out.

Please don't misunderstand. I'm not saying that my refusal to read reversals is the only way to go here. I'm only suggesting that you try it for yourself and see what happens. You may just discover that you have no personal need for the extra hassles, and that the time spent on reading reversals is well used elsewhere.

Quick Answers to Yes and No Questions

Sometimes, we just need a few answers. Not anything detailed, not anything fancy. We just need to know whether we're on the right track or not. And for these types of questions, a simple "yes" or "no" will do.

For those cases, shuffle the deck thoroughly while concentrating on the question. Then begin to lay the cards out faceup, one on top of the other. If you turn up an Ace, stop and begin another pile. If no Ace appears, continue to add cards until you have thirteen. Repeat the process until you have three stacks of cards.

Once the cards are in place, take a good look. If three Aces appear, the answer is a definite "yes." If none appear, the answer is "no." But what if only one or two Aces grace you with their presence? It simply means one of two things: either you weren't totally focused on the subject matter at hand, or an answer wasn't available based on the current question. Not to worry. Just clear your head and reformulate the question into simpler, more specific terms. Then try again. The answer you seek will be forthcoming.

Reading for Others

You may not have thought about reading for other folks when you purchased your deck. Maybe you just wanted to work with the cards, understand their meanings, and discover the personal path to empowerment. Perhaps it was simply an area of spirituality that you wanted to explore for yourself.

Once you have a deck in hand, though, one of two things is bound to happen. You're either going to be deluged with requests to teach the Tarot, or someone's going to demand a reading. And no matter how you slice it, you're not going to feel ready for either.

The first request is easy enough to pass off. Since you've only just begun to explore the system, there's no possible way you could know enough to teach it to anyone else. People will understand that and let it go.

Unfortunately, the second can present a problem. No matter how much you protest—or how carefully you explain your lack of skill—someone will invariably persist. And in this case, just saying "No!" won't help. If you don't believe me, try it once and see what happens. I guarantee that you'll suddenly transmute from the wonderful, loving person whom everyone knows you are, into some horrid, self-centered jerk who cares nothing for the well-being of others. It's a done deal, and there's absolutely nothing you can do about it. Except, of course, shuffle the cards and read.[3]

This really isn't such a bad thing, though. Even if you don't have a clue about the card meanings, reading for others forces you to trust yourself and your guide. It also allows you the practice necessary to master the system. And since you've already explained that you're just a beginner, you won't be expected to read with complete accuracy. They're happy, you come out smelling like a rose, and everybody is a winner.

Even so, that nagging feeling of "I'm not good enough to do this" is bound to creep in. I know what I'm talking about here. How? Because I've been there and done that. Here's what happened:

Shortly after I began working with the Tarot, a friend of mine came over with a proposition. The gist of it was that the manager of the bar in which she worked was looking for something special to draw customers in for Halloween, and she'd suggested that I read cards. The readings would be free to the customers, but I could put out a tip jar. And to sweeten the pot, he was offering three hundred dollars cash for four hours of work over a two-night stint.

I was stunned. While the money sounded good—and I certainly could have used it at the time—there was no way I could do it. I explained that I didn't have enough experience, that I couldn't possibly be accurate, and that I couldn't even begin to help anyone else solve their problems. At that particular point in my life, I was having lots of trouble just solving my own.

Fortunately for me, though, she wouldn't take no for an answer. She said that I could put a "For Entertainment Purposes Only" notice on the reading table so I wouldn't have to worry about accuracy. The readings would only be ten minutes long. And since the gig was for happy hour—the noisiest time of the day—it was doubtful that my "clients" would even be able to hear the whole spiel. Looking at it from that angle, it was an offer I couldn't refuse.

I arrived at the bar on the appointed day. Nothing could have prepared me for what I found, however. There, in front of my table, were at least twenty people lined up—and they were all waiting for readings! I wanted to run from the room, disappear into thin air. Maybe even just dissolve into the floor. Since none of those were real options, though, I just choked back my fears, grabbed some gumption, and sat down. Then I began to read.

What happened next was one of the most incredible experiences of my life. For the very first time, I knew exactly what the cards meant. I knew precisely what to say, when to say it, and how to phrase it. As the hours sped past, I became more and more accurate. I was amazed. The customers were amazed. And my tip jar showed the proof. After the first hour, it actually overflowed onto the table!

Here's the deal. Being "forced" into reading for others was the best thing that ever happened to me. And it can be for you, too. So when someone asks you to read for them, just choke back your fears and grab those cards. What you discover won't just amaze you—it will change you forever.

Reading for Yourself

While reading for others can be fun—and can also you to better understand the Tarot—the opposite is often true of reading for yourself. After reading this last statement, it's fair to say that you probably think I've lost my mind. After all, you bought a Tarot deck to learn about the system. You bought this book to learn how to use the cards for personal empowerment. And if you can't read the cards for yourself, how in the world are you going to do either? It's a viable question. But before you put this book down and close it forever, just hear me out. Doing so can save you tons of trouble in the long run.

While it's easy to be objective about other people's situations, human nature comes into play when we look at our own. This is because we're too close to the situation. We know all the players. We've already formed personal opinions. And that being the case, emotions can't help but come to the forefront. Trying to disassociate ourselves to the point of being objective is difficult at best. In fact, it's damned near impossible.

But even knowing that doesn't stop us. We forge ahead anyway, taking all those personal feelings and opinions and coupling them with a spread. (After all, we should know what's going on, and the cards will tell us, right?) Since the same cards can mean many different things—and personal objectivity is obviously lacking here—we no longer have a "what you see is what you get" situation. Instead, we look for loopholes. We desperately search out the best case scenario. It's only human nature at work. But unfortunately, it doesn't make for a very accurate reading.

With that said, I think it's much more effective to have someone else read for you—especially if you really need some solid advice. This is not to say that you shouldn't practice your reading skills, or maybe even draw a card every morning to get a general idea of how your day will go. All it means is that unless you can be as objective about your own life as a stranger on the street would be, your natural intuition can become overshadowed by personal delusion. And personal delusion is something we can all do without!

Endnotes

1. Some scholars believe that the word "Gypsy" is a derivation of the word "Egyptian." Others insist that the Gypsies originated in Europe, and that they had absolutely no connection with the Egyptian world or culture.

2. These cards are known today as the Major Arcana.

3. For reading spreads, see appendix D in the back of this book.

2

The Cards

What most people don't realize about the Tarot is that it's much more than a deck. Instead, it's a system that just happens to be comprised of cards. And there's a reason it's divided up the way it is.

The Major Arcana cards—or trumps—are numbered 0 through 21. And when placed in order, they outline the journey of life's path. The journey itself starts and ends with the Fool, the character who represents each of us as we go about the business of seeking and absorbing knowledge.

Now before you get all bent out of shape, understand that the Fool isn't some moronic idiot. He doesn't represent some mental inadequacy or learning disability. He simply isn't aware of all there is to learn; and as such, he's an empty vessel just waiting to be filled. In fact, once you get to know and understand him, you'll find that he's a pretty cool character—one that you'll be proud to call your representative.

But before we jump feet first into the personal journey, there are a few things you need to understand about the Major Arcana, especially when it comes to their frequent appearances in card spreads. For one thing, they represent things that affect us but are beyond our control. We often—even when minding our own business—find ourselves firmly ensconced in situations that we didn't initiate, and wouldn't have normally touched with a ten-foot pole. Still, there we are—floundering about and looking for a reasonable solution.

Here, the Major Arcana cards remind us that the tangled mess at hand is not our fault—something good to know when life seems to be plagued with chaos—rather, it came from a set of steps devised to teach a personal lesson. The final outcome, of course, is solely up to us. And how we handle the problem will definitely affect any future twists and turns on the personal path.

While these cards always shed light on situations that we don't understand, their power goes even further. In short, they remind us that we are never alone on the personal path, that unseen forces are always at work to help or hinder us along the way. And once we understand that, two things happen. First, we realize that we are not necessarily at fault for every aggravation encountered. Second, and more important, we begin to understand that we are not personally responsible for every stroke of good luck that comes our way. Instead, we begin to see the strokes of luck for what they are: pats on the back bestowed by a Higher Power, and gifts that give us the impetus to keep moving and growing as we strive toward completing our personal journeys. That having been said, let's get started!

The Journey of the Major Arcana

While the journey in question starts with the *Fool*, he isn't really a fool at all. In fact, nothing could be further from the truth. He comes into this life with all the knowledge of the Universe, and because he's had no dealings with societal expectations, he's open to all around him. Simply put, he has no fear. He's willing to do or try anything, just to see what happens.

That's all well and fine. But if the Fool already has all knowledge at his fingertips, what's the point of the journey? Isn't it a waste of time? No. The problem is that the Fool has no idea what to do with the knowledge he possesses. He has no clue how to use it, how to apply it, or how to make it work for the good of all. He simply doesn't have the wisdom of experience. And that's what the journey is all about.

The Fool starts off skipping along the path, smiling in simple wonder at the beauty around him. He doesn't get far, though, before he meets the *Magician*. This is an important acquaintance, for not only is the Magician a clever sort who's in complete control of the Elements, the Universal workings, and the powers of manifestation, he knows how to engage them for the good of all. And after some discussion, he decides to teach his new friend. Before long, the Fool not only learns how to change his own reality, but the reality of others along his path. And in doing so, he learns the importance of wisdom.

Of course, this leads him to the *High Priestess*—for while Universal manipulation falls within the realm of the Magician, all mysteries are within the High Priestess' domain. Here, the Fool learns about unseen forces, the balance of light and dark, and the joys of the spiritual world. He learns to trust what he cannot see, cannot hear, and cannot hold. And while he understands this realm perfectly, he cannot comprehend the warmth now stirring deep within his heart.

For this reason, the High Priestess sends him on to the *Empress,* the keeper of unconditional love. It is at this point that the Fool begins to experience the joys of nurturing encouragement, and really begins to grow. For under the tender care of the Empress, he learns that the seed of life is love—that wondrous thing that blossoms in his heart—and that all creation and abundance comes from its sowing. The only problem is that he's not really sure about what to do with it.

That brings him to the *Emperor,* the master of wise advice. And because the Emperor's been there, done that, and wears the tee shirt as proof, he easily explains the process. That's not all, though. He also explains that other things—responsibility for one's actions, a fair amount of give and take, and a willingness to improve oneself—are necessary to live in the real world. The Emperor goes on to teach him about assembling facts, the importance of sound judgment, and the value of good decision-making. And while this is all within the Fool's sense of understanding, he still has no real grasp of why things are the way they are.

Because this is not within the Emperor's realm, he sends the Fool to meet the *Hierophant*. And it is here that the Fool first encounters fear—the fear of embarrassment, the fear of judgment, and the fear of peer pressure—for the Hierophant introduces him to society and its expectations. He comes to understand tradition (however mindless it may be), status, and convention. But the Hierophant complicates matters a bit. He reminds the Fool to never lose sight of who he really is, regardless of what others expect—for only then can he remain true to his own individual life purpose.

Confused but determined to figure things out, the Fool then happens upon the *Lovers*. This only serves to frustrate him further, for while they move separately, they also move as one. It is here that he comes to understand where love—that wonderful seed within the realm of the Empress—really takes root and grows. And that while one can hold on to personal individuality, the joining of two hearts makes life's trials and tribulations much more bearable. The only problem is that in order to love someone this way, certain risks are necessary—the biggest, of course, being rejection and the possibility of a broken heart.

And since he doesn't quite understand, he hurries along the path until he sees the *Chariot*. At this point, he comes to see that action is always necessary to achieve one's desires—regardless of the risk involved. He understands that the ride may be bumpy, the ride may be smooth, the ride may take so many twists and turns that it takes all the gumption one can muster just to hold on. But none of that matters. All that's important is the initial decision to board the Chariot, and the courage to follow through.

So, the Fool jumps in the Chariot and continues the journey until he comes to a fork in the road. One horse goes this way, the other goes that way. And suddenly, the Chariot tips over, tossing the Fool at the feet of *Strength*.

Of all the people he's met on his way, this one confuses the Fool the most. For rather than the brute force he expected, she is a gentle, caring, unassuming soul. And when the Fool questions her power, she explains that real strength—the sort that moves mountains and rules countries—is very subtle in nature. It's calm and peaceful. It's often found in silence, and in the ability to allow others to make their own mistakes. But the Fool, of course—being the seeker that he is—wants to know where it comes from. And since she can't answer, Strength sends him on to the *Hermit*.

It is during his chat with the Hermit that everything begins to fall into place for the Fool. Together, they embark on an inner journey—a journey through the quiet recesses of the mind and spirit—and he discovers that strength comes from deep down inside. But that's not all. He discovers that the rest of what he's looking for is housed there, too, and that if he can't find it within, he'll never find it anywhere else. Satisfied and tired, he settles in, quite sure that his journey is over.

The Hermit, however, knows better. He sends the Fool in search of the *Wheel of Fortune*. Here, the traveler learns the importance of transformation, and the laws of spiritual gravity. He begins to understand that life is a series of up and downs, and that change—while not always pleasant—is always necessary. But even as he spins with the Wheel, constantly growing and changing, he questions the fairness of it all. He simply can't understand why good fortune seems so fleeting and discomfort lasts so long. And since the Wheel simply spins without answer, the Fool journeys on in search of *Justice*.

When he comes upon the scales, though, he's more frustrated than ever. But since he knows that there's a lesson to be learned somewhere, he settles in to watch for a bit. The scales tip and turn, move this way and that. And as each load is weighed, measured, and accounted for, he finally gets a clue. While life doesn't always seem fair, he comes to understand the real need for a system of checks and balances. Without them, he reasons, life, itself, wouldn't be worth living.

With that in mind, he moves on, understanding somehow that the lessons in balance have just begun. And when he encounters the *Hanged One*—suspended in mid-air and bobbing about with his foot caught in a rope—he knows that he's right. For upon offering to help his new acquaintance, the Hanged One declines. He explains that one must learn to live equally in both the physical and spiritual worlds; that too much time spent in one realm or the other throws things out of whack. Since the Fool understands this, he starts to leave. But the Hanged One calls after him with some last minute advice: never be so spiritually bound that you're of no earthly good. And it's this advice he ponders as he trudges along the way.

Of course, it all becomes clear when the Fool meets up with *Death*—for even though he looks scary, the traveler knows he must move forward to complete the journey. So he puts one foot in front of the other and goes forward to embrace his new friend. It's a good thing, too. For in the embrace, the Fool comes to understand that Death isn't frightening at all. And while it does, indeed, bring the end of all things, it also brings all new growth, infinite beginnings, and the realm of limitless possibility. So, armed with the power of rebirth and a head filled with vision and desire, the Fool waves goodbye and hurries along the path.

It's not until he meets *Temperance*, though, that he understands fully how to handle his newfound power, for it's here that he learns about a different kind of balance and self- control. He comes to understand that nothing is truly good or bad. That it's important to grab what life has to offer. But how it's used and in what amounts really makes a difference.

Contemplating the wonders of moderation, the Fool continues along his merry way, skipping and laughing and stopping to smell the flowers. Suddenly, though, he stops dead in his tracks. He has just spotted the *Devil*—a much more terrifying visage than even Death could manage. His heart filled with trepidation, he creeps closer—one step at a time—for he understands that there's something to learn from everyone on the path. And if he stops now, it's a sure bet that he'll never finish the journey.

Of course, the Devil thinks this is hilarious, for he knows he's anything but scary. Snorting and chortling and laughing with glee, he beckons the Fool onward until they're finally standing face to face. It is here that the Fool learns that the Devil is only a character conjured in the mind's eye, and that humankind, alone, gives him power. He discovers that it is the inability to accept what life has to offer that makes him grow, that it's the greed factor that makes him strong. And that if he'd only see himself as valuable and refuse to sabotage himself, that the Devil would simply disappear into thin air.

Thrilled with his newfound knowledge—and the fact that he's still in one piece—the Fool travels on until he hears an explosion. He runs toward the noise, certain that someone needs his help. What he finds, though, is nothing of the sort. It's only the *Tower* doing its thing—and it's now in the throes of complete and utter self-destruction. Drawing upon the lessons of the Devil, the Fool suddenly sees the problem. While the Tower is a mighty building, the foundation is faulty. In fact, the whole device is built on sand—and that being the case, it can't ever expect to stand the test of time. From this, the Fool learns that everything worthwhile—relationships, in particular—must be built on solid ground. This means honesty, trust, and the ability to go through life while remaining true to oneself.

And so, the Fool moves on—wandering this way and that—until he comes upon such incredible beauty that he just has to stop for a moment and stare. The object of his awe is the first *Star* of the evening, and he watches it rise in the moonlit sky. Completely enthralled, he questions its beauty and how it came to be. And through the conversation, he comes to understand that life is more than a series of tests—it is also a path where wishes and dreams and desires come true. He only has to want something so badly that he becomes one with the effort, channels his energy toward that goal, and asks the Star to make it happen. He decides to give it a shot. He makes a fervent wish, and starts back toward the path.

He can't help turning to look back at the Star, though. And as he does, another beautiful object comes into view: the *Moon* in all her splendor. Huge and full, and weaving her hypnotic spell, she seems close enough to touch. And the Fool, not understanding, can't resist the urge to embrace her. No matter how far he reaches or how hard he tries, though, all he gains is emptiness. From this he learns that life is not always as it appears, that it pays to be aware of the facts and keep them close by, and that while life is beautiful and precious, it also provides a treacherous trap—the trap of self-deception—the most common peril found along the path of life.

The sky darkens to blackness as the Fool hurries along the way. Then suddenly all is bright again. The source of the light is the *Sun,* a great fiery orb rising high in the sky. Of course, the Fool knows better than to reach for him—he remembers what happened with the Moon— but he simply can't resist the urge to bask in his light and smile at his wink. In fact, wandering in the gentle warmth lightens his step, fills his heart, and makes him feel good all over. At this point the Fool begins to understand the true gift of the Sun and its meaning. Simply put, it is success and all that it entails. The Fool comes to know that success is what comes from crossing hurdles and slaying fears, and coming out no worse for the wear.

So the Fool travels on feeling pretty good about himself. In fact, armed with the warmth of the Sun, he decides that he's the greatest creation ever invented. Everyone else is surely beneath him. He continues to revel in his newfound arrogance until, at last, *Judgment* knocks him on his butt. It is here that the Fool discovers the importance of listening to the inner voice—that tiny little whisper that keeps him mindful of other people's feelings, what is fair and what is not—and its gentle reminder to help those much less fortunate than he. And since he now understands that the power of success must always be tempered with a deep sense of right and wrong and a sense of respect for those around him, the Fool resumes his journey.

It isn't until the Fool comes across the *World,* though, that everything begins to make sense. He begins to see that the message of every character that crossed his path—from the Magician to Judgment—is woven together one into the other, and that their messages and advice have brought him to where he now stands. For with their help, the Fool has achieved the ultimate—he has evolved into the best he can be—and has reached the end of his long and drawn out journey. With much effort and sheer determination, the Fool has reached the World—the ultimate goal—and the realm of all attainment. And what he does with it now is solely up to him.

The Minor Arcana

Now that we've traveled the journey of the trump cards, it's time to take a look at the Minor Arcana. Often called the suits, these cards are divided into four sections— Rods, Swords, Cups, and Pentacles—with each section corresponding to a particular element and its direction. Just as nothing is cast in stone with the advice of the Tarot, such is the case with these correspondences. The suit of Swords, for example, is often coupled with air. Why? Simply because of the blade's abilities to slice through air and sail to its destination. I, however, disagree with this theory. My reasoning is that swords are forged of metal, and as such, a great deal of heat is necessary to provide a strong blade. Looking at it from this angle, the suit of Swords would definitely live within the realm of fire.

So, who's wrong? Who's right? More to the point, does anyone really know what the original creators of the system intended?

To start with, no one's wrong . . . but no one's right, either. The Tarot simply isn't built that way. It works because it flexes with your own personal individuality, and fluxes to fit your spiritual path. It's a simple matter of whatever seems right to you. With that in mind, feel free to adjust the following correspondences as you see fit. After all, this is your path we're talking about. And whatever feels right to you is the way you should go.

But I digress. The one thing that is cast in stone with the Minor Arcana is their role in the system. Simply put, these cards represent the events in life that fall well within our control: our achievements, our mistakes, our joys and miseries.

More important, though, they give us a clear and objective picture of who we are and where we stand. But that's not all. They also outline the steps we took to reach the final outcome. And this is excellent information to have on hand. Why? Because once we realize how we got from point A to point B, we can make informed choices. We can duplicate the steps that brought success. We also have the advantage of knowing why other steps resulted in disaster. This knowledge not only eases life's journey, but keeps us from making the same mistakes over and over again. Furthermore, it reminds us that responsibility for our own actions—something we often forget—is imperative when it comes to walking the personal path. And that's a reminder we simply can't do without.

That having been said, let's get started! Remember, though: if a particular correspondence isn't comfortable for you, just change it to fit your needs. It's the only way you'll be able to use the system to its best advantage. And that advantage is necessary to bring enlightenment along the personal path—the path you call your own.

Rods

The suit of Rods belongs to the element of air, and symbolizes its force within our lives. And on a mundane level, air is something we just can't do without. In fact, since it provides the oxygen that we breathe, we depend on it for our very lives. But there's more: it cools and refreshes, and keeps the Sun's overpowering warmth from burning the earth and its inhabitants. We depend on it to carry light, sow seeds, and prevent the soil from packing into impenetrable hardness. It also controls other things we seldom think about: our sense of sound, our sense of smell, and, to a large degree, our sense of taste.

On another level, though, air provides much more. It's responsible for the communication process. It breeds thoughts and ideas, fuels the flow of inspiration, and is the matrix from which all creativity abounds. And because of this, it also provides us with a plethora of beginnings, fresh starts, and new perspectives.

A spread comprised of many Rods—often depicted as budding branches—provides us with the many wonders of life. It brings us fresh activity, productivity, and new hope for the future. It reminds us that while life is an ever-changing, constantly evolving process, we are on the right track. All we have to do is stay the course, allow air's gentle breezes to clear the path, and use the inspiration gained to quicken the journey.

Swords

For the reasons discussed earlier, I associate the suit of Swords with the element of fire. Ruled by the Sun, we see fire everywhere we look. It's in the sunshine and starlight. It's in the dance of the candle flame. Appearing as electricity, nuclear power, and laser light, it eases our lives and helps us along our way. That's not all, though. It invisibly feeds the sparks of human passion by fueling our personal desires, moving us toward our goals, and, finally, bringing us to victory. It's something we just can't do without.

As important as fire is to us, though, it also has its downside. Because of its tremendous energy, it isn't easily restrained. This means that it can burn out of control. And when that happens, the very same properties—those that are normally so beneficial—can scorch, scar, maim, and destroy.

For these reasons, Swords signify the need for aggressive action. They remind us to protect ourselves against impending danger. They remind us to defend our positions and our belongings. But most important, they keep us mindful that because this power is double-edged, it must be wielded carefully. Without the use of caution and wisdom, there is no victory. We only succeed in cutting our own throats.

Cups

The suit of Cups belongs to the element of water, the source of all life. On a mundane level, water cools and contracts. It refreshes and cleanses. Sometimes it even stagnates. Its natural forms are many—rain, ice, snow, fog, dew—and all are important. It also keeps our bodies functioning properly by providing sweat, tears, and the liquid necessary for proper blood flow. In fact, if it weren't for water, all life—human, animal, and plant—would simply cease to exist.

The Moon rules the element of water, but it also rules something else just as important: our hearts and our feelings. For this reason, Cups not only represent all human emotion, but are said to form the heart of the Tarot. This means that they mirror our every feeling—remorseful sadness, romantic happiness, or even that occasional jealous rage—and lend it credence.

For this reason, it's a good idea to remember that every emotion we encounter has a downside, and that it's the way we handle our emotions that matters. Since our range of emotions can rise and fall and create hairpin curves in our lives, we need to proceed with caution. It's only with sure-footing that we can hope to successfully progress along the personal path.

Pentacles

Associated with abundance and plenty, Pentacles represent the fertility of the earth. Her gifts are many. She offers rich soils to nourish the plant life that provides food and beauty. She offers conveniences like wood, paper, glass, metal, and an assortment of other gifts necessary for our survival. But for all that, she offers something else much more important: a solid base on which to live, work, and play.

Since the earth element comes from a combination of air, fire, and water in their most solid forms, Pentacles draw on all of the elements for their wealth. They denote fruitfulness and abundance. They speak of opportunities, business matters, success, and general good fortune. But that's not all. They also bring financial windfall, status, and accomplishment. For these reasons, Pentacles are always a welcome sight in any spread.

Just as the earth is rich, though, know that it also has drawbacks. It can manifest in stagnation and laziness. Too much can even bring on severe cases of stubbornness. So remember to keep your mind on your business. Pay attention to all that's going on around you. And above all, take steps to protect the good fortune that the Pentacles bestow. Otherwise, it can all be blown away a bit at a time—like particles of dust twirling on the wind.

Court Cards and Numerical Cards

Just as the Minor Arcana is divided into four suits, each suit is separated into two sections—court cards and numbered cards—with each section having its own purpose. The court cards are those that depict kings, queens, knights, and pages. These images are important because they rule the suit, and help us to understand its significance within the system. Sometimes they represent people who play significant roles in our lives. At other times, they simply reflect the keys that unlock the events at hand. At any rate, they hold an essential place in the system.

The numbered cards have their place, too. Taking their cues from the court cards of each suit, they signify cause and effect and the specific events that flavor our lives. This is important because it gives us insight into what happened, what went wrong, and what's necessary to put things back on an even keel. Without these cards, we'd have no way of knowing whether the current path is worthwhile, or whether we'd be better off changing course and delving into other areas. It's information that we simply can't do without.

As with the trump cards, each card of the Minor Arcana has its own meaning and purpose. And that discovery process is something I leave up to you. However, each card group—Kings, Queens, Aces, Twos, and so on—holds a common set of values that binds its members together, creating a sort of informational adhesive, if you will. And once understood, it's these truths that will open the door to an easy determination of the specific meanings of the group's individual cards. For your convenience, I've outlined them for you.

General Court Card Meanings

Kings

While this group is indicative of authority and expertise, it's important to note that the power of its individual members lies solely in the areas of their personal suits. The King of Pentacles, for example, is powerful when it comes to stability and financial gain, while the King of Cups is most masterful in matters of the heart. As a whole, though, this group is one of wise counsel, worldly rulership, and status. Its members may also signify particular individuals who play important roles in our lives.

Queens

Even though this group, like the previous one, holds the power of its individual suits, it has little to do with mundane authority. Instead, it holds dominion over our innermost feelings and controls that which we cannot see. The members of this group understand the importance of emotion, and the need to nurture, fertilize, and cultivate. They also hold the keys to the psyche, and remind us to listen for the inner voice and heed its advice so that we'll be able to develop the intuitive power necessary to understand our own personal mysteries.

This group may also represent specific people whom we meet on the personal path.

Knights

This group is one of action, and its members take their cues from the suits they represent. They rush headlong into conflict, for war-winning strategies are their strong point. Because they are driven by pure and unbridled energy, they often indicate where our powers lie, our personal focus, and the steps we're willing to take to achieve our goals. And while this group may also represent specific people, more often than not, these people act as harbingers of travel, adventure, and a major increase of personal activity.

Pages

The official errand runners of the royal family, this group acts as the messengers of the system. Their appearance signifies the need to study situations, come up with a plan of action, and take the steps necessary toward total resolution. This often involves taking a chance, a risk, or tampering with something we'd rather not mess with. However, it's the job of this group to show us that such action is not only essential to personal growth and development, but is also a necessary component in helping us to embrace further possibility. As with the other court groups, these cards may also symbolize people— but when that's so, they usually represent people who have not yet reached adulthood.

General Numerical Card Meanings

Aces

As the number "one" signifies the beginning, such is the case with this group. Ruling the self, Aces bring many types of personal births and initiations, as well as assorted opportunities. And because they often represent the seeding of personal potential, changes of perspective and new ways of looking at things are also within this realm.

Twos

This group is representative of Universal balance and duality. It speaks of a cooperative effort between opposites—male and female, dark and light, the spiritual and the mundane, and so on—and a working together of polarities to achieve successful results. Since personal intuition also comes to the forefront, it is sometimes seen as the stabilizing factor—the beginning of a balancing act, if you will—between the seen and unseen.

Threes

Just as the previous group speaks of cooperation, such is the case with this one. However, the focus here is usually on mundane teamwork to bring about the manifestation of personal goals and desires. This often means that help is on the way, and that friends and acquaintances will do their parts as long as you keep working diligently toward the effort at hand. The appearance of this group can also signify the ripening of a period of self-expression, and the cooperation of mind, body, and spirit toward making your dreams come true.

Fours

This group is very important because it indicates personal turning points and the stabilizing effects they have in our lives. It also speaks of the boundaries and limitations that we set for ourselves, the doors of opportunity that we allow to open, and the way we choose to bring personal projects to completion. The most stable of the numerical groups, Fours often act as the security guards of the Tarot.

Fives

Life is filled with a wide assortment of changes and alterations. Pleasant or not, these adjustments are always necessary for personal growth, and that's exactly what this group is all about. It outlines the personal challenges that cross our paths, and offers the insight necessary to deal with them as we continue the journey of daily living.

Sixes

A sensitive approach is important when this group appears, for it signifies that which we feel in our hearts. It speaks of love and harmony and emotional balance. It whispers of all that we hold dear. But more important, this group points out the ways that we manifest these things in our lives, and provides insight into appropriate steps to take as well as problem patterns that need revision.

Sevens

While this group certainly touts personal independence, there's more to it than that. It outlines the discipline necessary to mature into fully developed adults. It points out the work necessary for achievement, and the tenacity that's essential for successful results. No slouching allowed with this group. It is, without a doubt, the workhorse of the system.

Eights

Evolution and expansion hold the keys to this group. Often, they reflect a reevaluation period at hand, and a need to make changes both in personal priorities and perspectives. While these changes aren't always easy or comfortable, they provide the catalyst necessary for us to become who we were born to be. The only caution here is to remember that successful growth takes time and planning. That being the case, we must be careful not to bite off more than we can chew.

Nines

While this group definitely entails challenges, its common thread has very little to do with the obstacles at hand, or the cards that life deals us. Instead, it involves the way that we play our cards to meet those challenges, and how we handle related situations in order to achieve our goals. On a lighter note, this group also reflects good fortune and magical completion—and that's something we can never have enough of!

Tens

This group revolves around beginnings, endings, and the period of regeneration necessary to start anew. It also outlines cause and effect, and the acceptance of personal responsibility for both our actions and reactions. Anything associated with this group happens in a big way—so big, in fact, that it almost always takes our breath way. That being the case, be prepared when Tens come to call. Whatever they bring—positive or negative—will no doubt blow you away.

3

The Self-Discovery Process

No book on the Tarot would be complete without some sort of real explanation of how the cards apply in daily life, and this book isn't any exception. The material you'll find here, though, isn't the same kind you'll find elsewhere. The reason is two-fold. For one thing, this section is designed solely to help you on the personal path, and for that reason, we'll only look at the Major Arcana cards as they apply to you personally. Second, and just as important, card meanings have variables. They can vary from person to person, and spread to spread. This means that the same definitions don't always ring true. The Tarot simply isn't built that way.

I once had the opportunity, for example, to observe a reader with over thirty-five years of experience. Reading after reading, I watched her lay out the cards. I committed her every word to memory. At the end of the day, though, I had to admit that I was more than just a little confused.

The Hierophant card had come up several times during the course of the day. And each time, it seemed to have a different meaning. Once it was a religious figure. Another time it represented someone who was worried about what others might think. Before the day was done, it had also signified hidden talents, unspoken feelings, and an assortment of other things too numerous to mention.

It was its final appearance that really got me, though. As the reader turned up the card, she just giggled. And then, without batting an eyelash, she said, "Somebody in this relationship really likes kinky sex!" Of course, you could have knocked me over with a feather. That statement certainly wasn't one I'd have associated with the Hierophant—or with any other card in the deck, for that matter. It turned out, though, that the reader was right. And for the life of me, I just couldn't figure it out.

Fortunately, the reader helped me discover my problem. Though the card meanings do, indeed, have guidelines, there are no hard-and-fast rules. Think I'm kidding? Then take the Hierophant, for example. While it generally signifies a religious person or someone caught up in the trappings of societal thinking, that can cover a lot of ground. If a person is trying to live up to society's expectations, for example, that person may not show his or her true colors. Why? Because that person may be worried about what the rest of the world might think, may fear the discovery and development of a unique talent, or be afraid to speak out. Yes, that person might even worry about someone discovering that his or her sexual preferences don't meet societal expectations. And so that person lives a lie—exploiting himself or herself day after day—all for the sole purpose of trying to fit into a world that couldn't possibly understand him or her.

Looking at things from this angle, the Hierophant becomes extremely multifaceted—and it's no exception to the rule. The rest of the cards follow suit, each just as complex as the others. For this reason, two things are imperative when working with this chapter. First, take some time to meditate on the personal cards that follow. (For further information, please see the Card Meditation section in chapter 1.) Second, and perhaps more important, always go with your first impression, regardless of what I've listed in the following guidelines. Second-guessing yourself could lead you to believe something other than that which is true for you. And when working with self-empowerment, that which is true for you is all that matters.

The Spirit Card

While each of us has a reason for being born, our purpose is often less than clear. So we flounder about trying to figure out where we belong and why. Sometimes, we're successful. More often than not, though, we aren't. Why? Because we simply don't know where to go for help.

Fortunately, the Tarot can guide the way. All it takes is some simple addition and the Major Arcana cards from your deck.

Just add the digits of your birth date together. Take, for example, May 6, 1955. The equation looks like this:

$$5 + 6 + 1955 = 1966$$
$$1 + 9 + 6 + 6 = 22$$

In this case, the total is 22—the largest number we can use in this exercise. Reduce any number greater than 22 again. (The sum of 23, for example, is 5.) You get the idea.

Choose the Major Arcana card that matches your number (for 22, choose the Fool; its number is zero) and check out the Spirit card meanings and advice on the following pages. Then study the card carefully and go on to the meditation process. Remember to pay close attention to the messages you receive, for they will guide your spiritual path from this day forward.

Spirit Card Meanings and Advice

0 (22): The Fool

If this is your card, your Spirit simply begs for knowledge. And that being the case, it's your job to soak it up. Study, learn, and share your findings with others. Know that those who learn from you will have something to teach you as well.

1: The Magician

Should the Magician appear as your Spirit card, you have a very important purpose. You're here to solve problems, repair relationships, and turn situations around for the good of all. There's no need to become overwhelmed, though. Just fix one thing at a time, and know that the world will become a better place for your efforts.

2: The High Priestess

Connection is the key to the High Priestess. And when it appears as the Spirit card, it signals a direct link between the worlds of spirit and mundanity. Know that you are the conduit from which all information flows, and it's your job to help others stay balanced between the two realms.

3: The Empress

If the Empress is your Spirit card, you were born to nurture others. It's up to you to support goals, fertilize dreams, and help them to blossom into reality. Your mission is also one of unconditional love. Remember, though, that this sort of love never assumes or binds. It flows, instead, on a steady course—constant, fluid, and all-encompassing.

4: The Emperor

When the Emperor appears as the Spirit card, it's your job to advise. That being the case, always look at every angle of a situation before opening your mouth. If you must be critical, be constructive. In doing so, you'll ease the path of others as they travel life's journey.

5: The Hierophant

Although the Hierophant is usually seen as a nonconformist of sorts, in the position of the Spirit card, it denotes the ultimate explorer. This means that it's up to you to present options, possibilities, and fresh perspectives to those who wouldn't ordinarily see them. This is, by no means, an easy job. Know, however, that it is an important one in the Universal scheme of things.

6: *The Lovers*

When the Lovers appear as the Spirit card, your mission falls within the realm of relationships—both intimate and otherwise. It's your job to help others not only see the value of commitment, fair play, and constant communication, but to help them follow through. It doesn't stop there, though. The other part of your mission is to point out any harmful relationships, and give others the courage to end them.

7: *The Chariot*

When it comes to the Tarot, the Chariot is the ultimate mover and shaker. Falling in the position of the Spirit card, though, its mission is one of completion. That being the case, it's your job to help others take action and follow through—even in seemingly impossible situations. In doing so, you will not only help them to understand that nothing is unattainable, but give them the courage to move forward on their chosen path.

8: *Strength*

Strength in the position of the Spirit card has nothing to do with brute force. Instead, it's a matter of helping others stand up for their beliefs, and what they feel is right and wrong. There's also another side to the coin here, though. It's also up to you to help them see when their beliefs are flawed, to give them the courage to admit it, and to assist them in stepping down from the soapbox before others follow their lead.

9: The Hermit

When the Hermit appears as the Spirit card, it means that you are the keeper of the Universal light. And as good as it sounds, it's not an easy job. Why? Because your mission is not only to help instill self-confidence and self-worth in others, but to convince them to let their personal lights—talents, abilities, and so on—shine forth to guide the rest of the world. Know that by doing your job well, you'll do more than help those around you see their personal value—you'll make the world a better place to live.

10: The Wheel of Fortune

The Wheel of Fortune spins in constant motion, and if this is your Spirit card, you probably feel like you're on a merry-go-round with no chance of stopping. This is normal, for it's your job to help others handle the ups and downs of everyday living. Celebrate when they're on top. Speak words of encouragement when they're down. And always keep them mindful of the turning wheel— for when things hit bottom, there's no place to go but up again.

11: Justice

If Justice is your Spirit card, you were born with a natural sense of fair play. That being the case, it's your mission to point out when others have gone too far, or when they need to back off and reevaluate. But that's not all. It's also important to lend encouragement to those who have difficulty standing up for themselves. Only then will they get a fair shake and receive the justice they so sorely deserve.

12: The Hanged One

In the Spirit card position, the Hanged One represents the balance between the mundane world and that of spirit. This means that it's up to you to help others see the importance of both. Too much of one or the other, and life becomes difficult. Helping them to strike an equal balance will not only make their lives easier, but bring a feeling of accomplishment you've never attained before.

13: Death

Of all the cards in the Major Arcana, Death is, perhaps, the most misunderstood—especially when it comes to its appearance as the Spirit card. Your mission here has nothing to do with death at all. Rather, it's up to you to point out when it's time to stop, when it's time to start over, and when it's time to bring fresh ideas into play. This is a very important job in the Universal Plan, for without your help, the realms of reality and spirituality would truly cease to exist.

14: Temperance

Patience, moderation, and simplicity are key when Temperance arrives as the Spirit card. And in our fast-paced world of "more is better," that makes your mission very important. For this reason, actively search out ways to help others understand that they should never settle for what's available, for that which is worthwhile is always worth waiting for. It's also important to show them that a simple life—void of societal and material trappings—makes the path of life much easier to tread.

15: The Devil

Like Death, the Devil card is very misunderstood—especially when it comes to the Spirit card position. Simply put, your mission involves teaching others to grab the good in life, and to understand that they deserve it. This often takes some doing, though, since human beings tend to sabotage themselves when extraordinary luck comes their way. In this case, it's your job to make them see that the Universe offers only what is necessary, and refusing its help is paramount to the proverbial slap in the face.

16: The Tower

When the Tower appears in the Spirit card position, your mission is that of mover and shaker. It's up to you to offer new ideas and fresh perspective even when it isn't popular. Know that it's often necessary to pull the rug out from under those who stagnate, for change—while seldom pleasant—is always imminent. And without it, humankind will cease to evolve. This makes your job very important, indeed.

17: The Star

The Star holds, perhaps, one of the most important Spirit purposes of all. Simply put, it is that of giving hope. That being the case, it's your job to help others to love themselves, and to feel good about themselves. Once you do, they'll realize that no personal goal—no matter how impossible it seems at the onset—is unachievable.

18: The Moon

When the Moon rises to the Spirit card position, it's time to make others aware of the changes going on around them. Help them to remove those rose-colored glasses, then present the facts. Only then will they be able to see the world as it really is. And only then will they be able to embrace the lives they were born to live.

19: The Sun

The Sun is a very fortunate card, indeed—especially when it falls within the realm of Spirit purpose. That's because its message makes your mission easy, fun, and enlightening. It's only up to you to convince others that the Ancients are smiling on them, that their success is imminent. And that being the case, all they have to do is reach out, grab it, and embrace all the happiness it has to offer.

20: Judgment

Judgment calls for a hands-on approach when it falls in the Spirit card position. That's because it's your mission to help others looks at both sides of the coin, and make decisions based on nothing more than the facts. Since human beings tend to be lead by their hearts rather than their minds, though, this is no easy task. While your work will be difficult, know that it's important—for only through your efforts will those around you learn to make firm decisions that will get them through life and ease its path.

21: The World

As with the Sun, you are fortunate if the World appears as your Spirit card. Why? Because completing your mission is only a simple matter of showing those around you that they are in a position to have whatever they want. All they have to do is ask. While this job can be fun and rewarding, understand that it's also up to you to let others know that any requests must be very specific. That's because the Universe only sees things in black and white, so it will only deliver an exact duplicate of that which is requested—nothing more and nothing less.

The Lesson Card

Just as our spirits have purpose, so do our lives. In fact, each lifetime that we're born into comes with a specific lesson. A lesson that—when properly learned and added to the sum of our previous lessons—brings us to the ultimate goal: that of spiritual evolvement and perfection.

But what if we don't know what this life's lesson is? What then? Not to worry. The Tarot can help here, too. Take the two digit total from the sum of your birth date (see page 58), then add the numbers together. For example:

22 = 2 + 2 = 4

In this case, 4 is the life lesson number. (If you don't have a two digit number, it just means that your spirit number and your life lesson number are the same.)

Once you have the number, find its corresponding card in the Major Arcana and begin the meditation exercise. If you're not getting the information you're looking for—or if none of it seems pertinent to your life lesson—ask direct questions. Listen carefully. The knowledge you receive will not only ease your lesson, but prepare you for any rough spots on the personal life path.

Lesson Card Meanings and Advice

0 (22): The Fool

A card of innocence, awe, and wonder, the Fool teaches that it's imperative to find the silver lining in even the darkest of clouds. Know that no matter how dismal things look, something wonderful is always on the horizon. It's just a matter of being able to see the whole picture. Admittedly, this isn't easy. But seeing life as an adventure—an exploratory exercise that allows you to stop and smell the roses along the way—can make it more enjoyable than you ever imagined.

1: The Magician

The Magician teaches that life is filled with possibilities, and it's up to you to grab or discard them as you wish. Don't like your current situation? Change it. Unhappy with your lot in life? Reinvent yourself. You are the master of your own destiny, and nothing—not even that which seems out of reach—is impossible for you. So, have what you want. Become who you wish. But remember that this sort of power only comes at a price: that of personal responsibility.

2: The High Priestess

The lesson of the High Priestess is that life is not always a "what you see is what you get" situation. That's because unseen forces often set up situations that we must deal with. While the circumstances, themselves, are often beyond our control, the manner in which we deal with them is not. For that reason, investigate all angles and keep your wits about you. Handle one thing at a time. And whatever you do, don't even think of bucking the Cosmic system. Just go with the flow and untangle each problem as it arises. Only then will life's journey provide an easy path.

3: The Empress

As the eternal mother, the Empress teaches the lesson of nurturement. But make no mistake, this lesson goes further than home, hearth, and family. It extends into the world around you and the people whom you invite into your life. If this is your card, it's also important to remember to pamper yourself. For unless you learn to love yourself and tend to your own needs, it's doubtful that you'll have the skills to bring that sort of tender loving care to anyone else.

4: The Emperor

The Emperor, as a father figure, brings the lesson of wise advice. And while the wisdom of experience will definitely help you here, it's important to remember that every situation is different. For that reason, present the facts to those who come to you. Then help them to look at every option and possibility before making a decision. Only then can you—the student—truly become the teacher, and go about the business of helping others along their way.

5: The Hierophant

The Hierophant teaches, perhaps, the most important lesson of all. It is, simply put, to be true to yourself. You are who you are. And that's enough, regardless of how others view you or what they expect from you. Know that it's okay to march to your own drummer. This doesn't mean, however, that you shouldn't strive to improve yourself or your personal circumstances. But in doing so, remember that any changes should be based on what's right for you, rather than because others deem it necessary.

6: The Lovers

When the Lovers card falls in this position, relationship lessons are at the forefront. And while intimate relationships may be involved, they only scratch the surface. With this lesson, it's important to understand the many facets of love and learn to express them all. This means embracing those we ordinarily might not. But even more important, it means learning to let go. And often, it's the latter that proves to be the hardest lesson.

7: The Chariot

The supreme card of action, the Chariot teaches us to get up, get moving, and get something done. This is not the time for procrastination, for situations at hand simply won't wait. While those with this lesson may often feel pulled in several directions at once, it's important to chart one course at a time and muster the courage to see it through. It's obviously not an easy path, but tenacity and personal endurance are the only things that will bring your goals to fruition.

8: Strength

Often misunderstood in this position, the Strength card does not promote brute force. Instead, it speaks of a quieter power—that sort of gentle strength that builds nations and rules worlds. Know that real accomplishment begins with a suggestion, builds with an agreement, and ends with a thorough follow-through. That being the case, learn to meet your goals by enlisting aid with the proverbial planting of the seed. It's okay for others to think it was their idea—or even take the credit. The strongest people often work behind the scenes and let others rest on their laurels.

9: The Hermit

When the Hermit comes to call in this position, it's time to come out of hiding, take center stage, and be recognized. Because you've worked quietly for so long, this may not be easy for you. Nonetheless, it's imperative that you learn to toot your own horn, and take due credit for your accomplishments. Understand that this has nothing to do with bragging or being boastful. Instead, it's a simple matter of accepting your rewards graciously, while pointing others in the direction of personal accomplishment.

10: The Wheel of Fortune

Should the Wheel of Fortune be your lesson card, know that your personal life path will be filled with a constant assortment of ups and downs. This isn't as bad as it seems, though. Without it, you would never know true appreciation. But more important, you would never come to understand that every situation—even the most grim—is nothing more than a window of opportunity. Know that the further along the wheel you spin, the closer you come to its blessings. And that those blessings—wondrous, though they are—are often born of trial and tribulation.

11: Justice

Justice brings the lesson of fair play when found in this position. Strive to be just, regardless of the cost. This is more than just knowing what's right and what's wrong, for when dealing with others, nothing is ever set in stone. Understand that extenuating circumstances attach themselves to every situation, and these, too, must be taken into account. For this reason, you must gather all information before forming an opinion, then follow through with a solution that is fair to everyone concerned.

12: The Hanged One

The lesson of the Hanged One is an important one, for it speaks of balance between the world of spirit and the realm of mundanity. To achieve this perfect balance, you must never be so spiritually bound that you're of no earthly good. At the same time, you must not allow the rigors of everyday life to completely consume you. Instead, find a happy medium. Give each world equal time. Only then will you be able to live happily in the two realms that make the whole.

13: Death

The lesson of Death is simple, but often difficult to learn. That's because it teaches that endings should be celebrated just as happily as beginnings—and as human beings, we just aren't wired that way. To that end, you may have to change the way you think. Understand that every ending brings a beginning, that with every death, there is new life. Once you begin to think in that direction, you'll realize that no ending is final; rather, it brings the gift of fresh starts, new beginnings, and limitless possibilities. And that is definitely worth celebrating.

14: Temperance

When Temperance falls in this position, it teaches the lessons of patience and moderation. Know that everything worthwhile is worth waiting for—and that nothing is gained from settling for less than that to which you're entitled. You also need to understand that there really can be too much of a good thing. This doesn't mean that you shouldn't grab what life has to offer. It just means that you should learn to exercise some self-control, for anything in excess can lead to exhaustion and illness on both the spiritual and mundane planes.

15: The Devil

Although the Devil card tends to frighten people, its message is anything but scary here. In short, it brings you the lesson of choices, and reminds you that how you play the game of life is solely up to you. Understand that you always have a choice—regardless of the situation at hand. It's just that life may deal you a hand you don't want to play. That having been said, take some initiative. Break damaging patterns. Learn to accept the good in life. Once you stop sabotaging yourself, life will provide a much smoother personal path.

16: The Tower

When the Tower falls in this position, it brings the lesson of relationship construction. Understand that nothing—not even the most well-constructed building—can stand for long if it's built on sand. Learn to build relationships from the ground up. Know that truth and trust are imperative from the first "hello." And if you always use them as major components in your foundation, the relationships you form will outlast the test of time.

17: The Star

While the Star speaks of wish manifestation, its lesson is of a more practical nature. It teaches that it takes more than mere wishing to make your dreams come true. That being the case, it's important to get up and get moving. Apply yourself. And, of course, do the necessary legwork. Otherwise, none of your dreams—no matter how badly you want them—will ever come to fruition.

18: The Moon

When the Moon falls in this position, it's time to rely on the advice your parents once gave you. In short: stop, look, and listen. Take off the rose-colored glasses. Pay attention to what's really going on around you. While it's good to see the best in the world, understand that turning a blind eye to the way things really are always results in personal downfall. Remember that forewarned is forearmed. Listen, too, to your inner voice. Heed its advice, and you'll never be caught off-guard.

19: The Sun

The Sun, in this position, brings the lesson of success. And while that may seem like no lesson at all, nothing could be further from the truth. Know that with success comes responsibility—not just for yourself and your actions, but for those who cross your path. Strive to be a good sport. Remember to help others along their way. In doing so, you'll find the real meaning of success and all it has to offer.

20: Judgment

When Judgment falls in this position, it's an indication that you must learn to lead with your mind and not with your heart. Know that every situation—no matter how complex—has a good and solid solution. You won't find it by dreaming your life away, though. Neither will it appear in the lines of a book. Understand that true solutions only come from studying the facts, engaging your brain, and using the common sense gained from past experiences.

21: The World

While the World brings the qualities of manifestation, completion, and infinite possibility, its lesson has nothing to do with resting on your laurels. Instead, it's one of personal service and reciprocation. In that case, be kind to those in less fortunate positions. Inspire others to greatness. Donate your time to service-oriented organizations, especially those that deal with the betterment of the planet. Only then can you evolve into the person you were meant to be.

The Talent Card

All of us are born into this world with a certain set of talents. Some talents gather immediate attention, and we usually use those to make a living. Others stay quietly in the background—and though they pop up once in a while—they seldom seem to have any real purpose. That being the case, we just pigeonhole them in the back of our minds and leave them there to catch our mental dust and grime.

That's a pity. Fact is, we aren't born with any talents that we truly don't need. Each one has purpose. Each one has meaning. And each one can help us in a way that no other can. The trick is in discovering how to use them and when.

For this exercise, simply match the day of your birth to the appropriately numbered Major Arcana card. (For example, a birthday of May 6 relates to 6, the Lovers. Use 0, the Fool, for 22, and reduce any numbers over 22 to a single digit.)

Once you have the card, use it for meditation. Ask questions about your talents. Find out what they are, why you have them, and what purpose they serve. Take notes. The answers are important—and you may need to refer to them later.

Talent Card Meanings and Advice

0 (22): The Fool

If the Fool is your talent card, your greatest asset is that of "no fear." This is because you know yourself well, and rely upon the lessons of past experiences to walk your path. You excel in ventures that involve uncharted ground and unexplored territory. As the Fool, you are the prime risk-taker.

1. The Magician

The Magician, in this position, brings the ability to make things happen. This means that you have a knack for amassing the facts and putting them together in such a way that something new and exciting develops. For this reason, you do well in ventures where inspiration is a key factor.

2: The High Priestess

When the High Priestess falls in this position, it indicates that you have the ability to cut through surface layers to find the source beneath. You not only enjoy investigation and research, but excel within their boundaries.

3: The Empress

Because the Empress is the eternal mother, she brings the talents of growth, abundance, and nurturement. This means that you do well with ground floor endeavors, or opportunities where you're able to watch your efforts take root and blossom.

4: The Emperor

Since the Emperor has been there, done that, and often wears the tee shirt as proof, he offers the talents of wisdom. For this reason, you do well in positions that require teaching skills or giving solid advice.

5: The Hierophant

Often seen as a symbol of the clergy, the Hierophant has a way of bringing the transformation necessary to live in the mundane world while grasping all that spirituality has to offer. And so your talents lie in any work that deals with the occult, spirituality, or the psyche.

6: The Lovers

While the intimate relationship is important to the Lovers, they also know that it takes teamwork to get by in the physical world. For that reason, you excel in service-oriented positions or those where partnerships are involved.

7: The Chariot

Moving at the speed of sound, the Chariot is driven only by the sheer will to reach its destination. Falling in this position, it brings you the ability to work well under pressure and to excel in fast-paced, fast-moving jobs.

8: Strength

Since the Strength card speaks of gentle power rather than brute force, its talents lie in people-oriented positions. For this reason, you'll excel in managerial positions, social work, or any other kind of work where dealing with the public is involved.

9: The Hermit

While the Hermit often works quietly behind the scenes, make no mistake: he also sheds light on every subject he studies. For that reason, his gifts are not only that of research and understanding, but the ability to impart that knowledge to others.

10: The Wheel of Fortune

Constantly spinning and infinitely turning, the Wheel of Fortune speaks of chance, risk, and the benefits thereof. As such, your talents lie in the ability to take a chance—even when the odds don't seem favorable—and still come out on top.

11: Justice

Often symbolized by the scales of balance, Justice knows what's right and wrong. In fact, it not only imparts a sense of fair play, but the ability to choose a favorable route when none are readily apparent. For this reason, you excel in positions where a firm voice of reason is necessary.

12: The Hanged One

The Hanged One has found the perfect balance between the world of humankind and the realm of spirituality. Even better, he knows what it takes to live in both worlds and manage it effortlessly. For this reason, your talents lie in counseling others and helping them to find the balance for which they seek.

13: Death

The mysteries of Death are endless, and that being the case, you are a multitalented individual. You will do best, however, in fields where discovery and new beginnings are at the forefront. Anything involving research, creation, science, or medicine are good bets for you.

14: Temperance

Even though we don't often think about it, Temperance makes the world go 'round. It balances chaotic flux with an even flow and brings all things together in moderation. For this reason, you're a "look before you leap" sort of person. This means that you do well in endeavors that require thought, caution, and careful planning.

15: The Devil

While the Devil never truly holds the reins in any situation, he can always make those around him believe that he does. For this reason, you excel in positions where you are in charge, and can delegate responsibilities. You also have the ability to be a good manager of people.

16: The Tower

Because the Tower reminds us that nothing can stand without a solid foundation, it is the card of reconstruction. That being the case, you have an eye for that which is necessary to make things work. You're also a natural at jobs that require building—both in the fields of construction and in the professional arena.

17: The Star

Since the Star is best known for its abilities to grant dreams and wishes, your talents lie in giving others hope. For this reason, you excel in positions where you work with people to boost their self-confidence, and help bring their goals to fruition.

18: The Moon

A mysterious but beautiful orb, the Moon holds dominion over constantly moving but unseen forces—the most important of which is the psyche. You not only work well with these forces, but explore their depths with ease. For this reason, you would make an excellent hypnotherapist, psychoanalyst, psychologist, or do well in any field where the inner journey is at issue.

19: The Sun

The most cheerful card in the Tarot, the Sun has reason to be happy. That's because he knows what it means to be successful. And if this is your talent card, so do you. For this reason, you know how to restructure things to make them work—even failing businesses—and turn them around so they meet with success.

20: Judgment

If Judgment is your talent card, you have the ability to look beneath the surface of any given situation and find underlying problems. Even more important, though, you always seem to find good, solid, and immediate solutions. For this reason, you excel in positions where extreme challenges and problem-solving are at the forefront.

21: The World

Because the World symbolizes what we hope to reach at the end of the personal journey, it is, in essence, the realm of limitless possibility. This means that you not only tend to reach for seemingly unreachable goals, but you also have the ability to bring them to fruition. For this reason, you do well in positions where the need to achieve the impossible is an everyday occurrence.

The Personal Year

Wouldn't it be nice to know what's in store for you from year to year? Maybe even just get a peek into the perks and challenges coming up? That way, you could stay one step ahead. You could make some plans. You might even be able to circumvent particular problems before they arise. It would not only make for an easier path, but also bring some order into areas of your life where chaos would otherwise surely breed.

While no tool can completely expose what's next to come, the Tarot can definitely shed some light on the subject. All you have to do is calculate your personal year. It's a simple process that will give you insight into what's coming up and what you need to look out for— and that's the sort of help we can all use.

To calculate your personal year, just add the month and day of your birth to the current year, and reduce. If your birth date, for example, was May 6, and the year you wanted to explore was 2003, the equation would look like this:

5 + 6 + 2003 = 2014
2 + 0 + 1 + 4 = 7

Since the number seven corresponds to the Chariot, that is the card for your personal year of 2003. Just look up the Chariot in the Personal Year Card Meanings and Advice section that follows, and you'll gain some insight into what's to come.

The only other thing you need to know about calculations is that double digit numbers should never be reduced any lower than 22—and that 22 is, as always, reserved for the Fool. For example, if you were working with the same birth date for the year 2015, the equation would look like this:

5 + 6 + 2015 = 2026
2 + 0 + 2 + 6 = 10

The number ten corresponds to the Wheel of Fortune. You get the idea.

Even though it seems logical that, with this system of calculating, all of the Major Arcana cards will appear in order over and over again, such is not the case. During the first forty years of my life, for example, I only experienced personal years 2, 3, 4, 10, and 17 once, and never had personal years that corresponded with the values of 1, 11, 12, 13, 14, 15, or 16. In fact, I won't even begin to experience most of those for another fifteen years or so. And some will never occur unless I live to be one hundred. The key phrase here is "personal year," and that's exactly what these calculations provide.

Just as particular values may never come up for you—or repeat themselves—neither do all personal years play out as you might expect. A Tower year, for example, may not provide a period when you change residences, or when your life seems to fall apart around you. Instead, it could be something much more subtle, like a time when you tie up loose ends and make plans for drastic changes. By the same token, you may not meet the love of your life during a Lovers year. You may simply find yourself in a state in inner reflection as you contemplate what you're really looking for in an intimate relationship. However, if you really study the aspects of the related card and do the meditation as described in chapter 1, you won't have many surprises. And major surprises are the one thing most of us want to avoid.

For this reason, some folks find it helpful to calculate their personal years far in advance. (Since the numbers generally run in ten-year cycles, they usually do it ten years at a time.) Others don't seem as concerned, and only calculate one year ahead. The choice is yours. But since I'm a "look ahead" sort of person, I figure my personal years by the decade. And I suggest that you do, too.

After all, forewarned is forearmed—and being forearmed can be extremely empowering.

Personal Year Card Meanings and Advice

0 (22): The Fool

The year of the Fool isn't anything like you may expect; in fact, it brings beginnings and fresh starts. You may move to another city, go back to college, or even start a new career. While a Fool year can be a bit disconcerting—and even somewhat scary—the key here is to relax. Embrace the new experiences and enjoy them. Only then can you reap their full benefit.

1. The Magician

A Magician year is very exciting, since it revolves around personal focus and taking whatever steps are necessary to reinvent yourself and/or change your current situation. You may find yourself tying up loose ends, completing projects that are long overdue, or maybe even ridding yourself of relationships that no longer work for you. You may also find yourself firmly ensconced in magical study, its benefits, and its realities. Either way, though, mind over matter will be at the forefront—and that's the very thing that will manifest the life you wish to live.

2: The High Priestess

The focus is on self during a High Priestess year. In fact, self-confidence is often on the rise, and with it, the discovery of an independence you've never known. You'll find that you not only have the ability to handle tasks that once seemed overwhelming, but that you can handle them with unexpected efficiency. This may also manifest in the urge to pamper yourself, especially if you've spent most of your life tending to the needs of others. Your intuitive powers may be on the rise as well. This year is about you—and anything even remotely related to self-discovery is at the forefront.

3: The Empress

The supreme nurturer, the Empress brings a period filled with issues of the home and hearth—and sometimes, even pregnancy. While women often bear children during an Empress year, the pregnancy factor can also be symbolic and could manifest in a newfound creativity of sorts. Latent artistic abilities may come to the forefront now. You may also feel the urge to nest, redecorate, or wrap yourself—and those you love—in luxury, pleasure, and beauty. Embrace the mother within, and spend this year doling out large doses of tender loving care. In doing so, though, remember to nurture yourself as well.

4: The Emperor

Since the keyword in an Emperor year is "structure," this can provide a very interesting period—especially to those who tend to live their lives in a disorderly, unorganized fashion. If this applies to you, you'll find a need to sort through, tidy up, and take care of business. If it doesn't, though, you'll still have plenty to do. With plans for the future at the forefront, you may find yourself breaking new ground and acting as a pioneer of sorts. On a personal level, this may also manifest in investing for the future, or even putting your will in order. However it affects you, though, the year is guaranteed to be filled with unlimited possibility. And firm, assertive action is necessary to get things done.

5: The Hierophant

While the Hierophant brings many lessons, this year can be very confusing. Why? Because it usually involves new understanding, a change of perspective, and a sudden urge to rid oneself of useless personal philosophies. For this reason, you'll probably find yourself listening and learning as a student, and being heard as a teacher. Old notions about society and its expectations fly out the window, and new ways to live within its boundaries emerge. With new ideas at the forefront, you may also find yourself taking a firm stand against issues that you previously supported. Don't worry about what others may think here. Know that stances often change through personal growth—and that it's only through these sorts of growing spurts that we finally understand who we are, what we are, and whom we can eventually be.

6: The Lovers

During a Lovers year, the focus is definitely on matters of the heart and related decisions. For this reason, you may suddenly find yourself madly in love, making personal commitments of an intimate nature, or deciding to get married. You may also choose to rid yourself of a relationship that's no longer working for you, give serious thought to what's really necessary for your happiness, then set off to make it happen.

Either way, though, these decisions will serve as turning points in your life, and taking responsibility for them will be just as important as the decisions themselves.

7: *The Chariot*

The Chariot, as always, brings constant motion and activity—but this is especially true when it rules the personal year. You're likely to find yourself changing residences, traveling to new places, and discovering a plethora of challenges along the way. That's not all, though. It also brings a proving period—a time when you must demonstrate your skills to the rest of the world, and prove that you have the capacity to handle anything that comes your way. It's a pretty tall order, but well worth the effort. For by working through the challenges of the Chariot, you'll add new skills to your repertoire—the most important of which is how to best protect yourself and others—as you continue upon life's journey.

8: *Strength*

As you might expect, the Strength year is designed to test your endurance in every sense of the word. And to complicate matters, you'll probably feel an urgency to create, start new projects, and get moving on ideas that have been on the back burner way too long. The problem is that there just isn't enough time. There's too much on your plate already, and it just keeps coming. The key here is not only to find a way to manage it all, but to handle everything in a productive, efficient manner. In doing so, you'll find an inner strength you never knew—and a sense of accomplishment that rivals no other.

9: The Hermit

A Hermit year is one of introspection and solitude. And that being the case, it involves getting to know who you really are. This can culminate in many ways. You may decide to take a sabbatical of sorts, and get away from the hubbub of everyday life. You may feel the need to simplify, get rid of things you no longer need, and end relationships that no longer work for you. You may also find yourself embracing a new course of study, developing previously hidden talents, or searching out a more personally suitable spiritual path. Whatever route this year takes, though, know that you'll emerge with a clearer view of who you are, where you're going, and who you may yet become.

10: The Wheel of Fortune

When the Wheel of Fortune appears as the personal year, know that you're in for quite a ride. Major changes—moves to other cities, changes of employment, drastic changes in personal perception, and so forth—not only occur at this time, but provide turning points that are guaranteed to impact the rest of your life. Fate enters the picture now, too, so you may find yourself dealing with an assortment of unusual situations, or—at the very least—those with which you have no prior experience. Once you get through them, though, know that rewards—fame, fortune, and extraordinary strokes of good luck—not only await you, but have a way of appearing from nowhere.

11: Justice

The personal year of Justice is just what its name proclaims: a period when fairness and balance are at the forefront and reign supreme. While this means that you're likely to work through some minor legal and financial issues—this could be as simple as signing contracts or changing the way you bank—during this period, there's more to it than that. Much more. You'll also be faced with deciding what's fair not only for you, but for those around you—and this could change the way you go about the business of day-to-day living. That being the case, make adjustments if necessary, but remember to stay true to yourself in the process. After all, a Justice year is about balance and if your needs don't figure in, the scales could tip right out of control.

12: The Hanged One

The personal year of the Hanged One is definitely about balance, but it also has to do with getting in touch with the real you. For this reason, you'll probably find yourself delving into personal issues, finding out why you feel the way you do, and taking a good hard look at the reasons for certain personal reactions. While some will be valid, others won't. And it's the latter that are important. You'll have to work through them and get rid of the hang-ups that are holding you back. It won't be an easy task. But when you've finally eliminated them from your life, your goals—even those that seem impossible—will once again be well within your reach.

13: Death

The Death year seldom involves anything scary. It can make for a difficult time, though. Why? Because it's human nature to hold on to everything that crosses our paths, and this year involves letting go of that which is no longer necessary. While this may be a simple matter of releasing material possessions, such is seldom the case. It's more likely that worn out notions, useless attitudes, and outdated perceptions are at stake. The value of certain relationships may figure in, too, so spend some time in evaluation mode. Decide what's important and what's not, then take steps to discard the old and useless. It's the only way to make room for the fresh, wonderful, and exciting things that await.

14: Temperance

While a Temperance year is one of restraint and self-control, it's also a year of caution and awareness. You may suddenly find yourself gathering facts and data—even if you're normally the impulsive type. You may also discover that there really can be too much of a good thing, and take some time to rethink your normal activities. The way you spend your time, money, and energy will probably come to the forefront here, and you'll find better ways to make use of each. No matter how this culminates, though, one thing is for sure: before it's said and done, you'll have learned the importance of moderation—and you'll also have picked up the creative problem-solving skills necessary to complete your path.

15: The Devil

No matter how you slice it, the Devil year is always difficult. Why? Because it simply gushes with personal power struggles, and everything they could possibly entail. You'll find them with your mate and your children. They'll occur with your friends, and the people you work with. And if that's not bad enough, you'll also feel them creeping up from deep inside of you and gathering momentum until they rage out of control. There is a way to get through this year successfully, though. You just have to remember not to sabotage yourself. Pick your battles well and think carefully before you act. The real victory here is in fighting for that which is really important, and letting go of the rest.

16: The Tower

If you're not prepared for it, a Tower year can leave you feeling a lot like Chicken Little. That's because everything—even the things you thought were most solid in your life—seem to come crashing down around you.

Tower energy can affect jobs, finances, relationships, and places of residence. It can even affect your personal values. The key here, of course, is to stay cool, calm, and collected—and search for the underlying causes. Once you find them—and you will—it's up to you to set about the reconstruction process. But in doing so, remember to rebuild carefully and systematically. A solid foundation never cracks. And if you build things correctly this time, you may never have to experience this energy again.

17: The Star

A Star year is always welcome because it involves getting credit for personal accomplishment. This means that you could find yourself on center stage winning awards, taking bows, and giving speeches. It could also play out in other ways. You may, for example, experience a period when everything you wish for is right at your fingertips. That being the case, it's a good idea to be careful what you ask for. Karmic rewards usually come into play, too, and strokes of good fortune await you everywhere you go. As exciting as this period is, though, remember to be kind to those less fortunate than you. Be humble in your success. And above all, give credit to others if it's due. How you handle this year will ease the path of personal years yet to come.

18: The Moon

Since an aura of mystery and secrecy has always surrounded the Moon, it's no surprise that it also applies to the personal year of the same energy. Previously hidden factors may surface now, giving you a clearer view of things going on around you. You may suddenly know what people are thinking—regardless of what they actually say. In any case, cutting through deception is at the forefront, and the power is yours. Often a Moon year brings vivid dreams, enhanced psychic ability, and the urge to explore personal spirituality. Don't push any of this aside. Learn to pay attention to your inner voice, and act on its advice. More to the point, embrace any new skills this year may offer. Then take the time to develop them. You'll need them later as you progress along your path.

19: The Sun

While a Sun year always brings a period of warmth and light, it also focuses on self-discovery. This doesn't always manifest in the ways you may think, though. That's because this sort of energy has little to do with inner journey. Instead, it brings your personal value and self-worth to light. That being the case, you're likely to discover that you really are an individual like no other, that you really do hold a special cord in the Cosmic web, and that your actions—no matter how miniscule—do, indeed, affect other people's lives. Along with this, you'll find a sense of empowerment that you've never known. And it's this newfound gift that will provide the courage to make the necessary changes for your personal growth and development.

20: Judgment

Evaluation is the key word when it comes to a personal year of Judgment. This means that you may find yourself looking at things with a fresh eye, and seeing angles that, before, were completely unapparent. With creative problem-solving skills at the forefront, too, you may even start to welcome the sorts of challenges that you once found impossible. On the flip side, this year could also bring some form of personal criticism; and if that's the case, you'll either find yourself standing up for your beliefs or reevaluating your personal positions. Either way, though, just remember to be true to yourself. Criticism—constructive or otherwise—doesn't necessarily constitute the difference between wrong and right.

21: The World

A personal year of the World is filled with awe and wonder. That's because it involves the process of discovery— and the object of its exploration is you! Since personal potential comes to the forefront now, you're likely to find yourself reaching higher than you've ever dreamed, and grabbing for that which seemed impossible only yesterday. Although anything is attainable now, you'll still have to work to set things into motion. You'll find, though, that the work involved isn't a problem. Your only limit during this period is the scope of your imagination. And that being the case, you can have it all; you just have to muster the gumption to bring whatever you want into reality.

Endnotes

The mathematical formulae contained in this chapter was first published in 1984 by Mary K. Greer in *Tarot for Your Self* (North Hollywood, Calif.: Newcastle Publishing, Inc., 1984).

Part Two

Tarot Magic

The Tarot's a system—a spiritual tool
Of power and symbols in the path of the Fool
A system of cards that forecasts what may come
When the path is continued with changes undone
Giving us warning and shedding its light
On personal patterns of wrong and of right
It's a system that teaches empowerment, too
And brings self-assurance to all that we do
But it's much more than that—more than any of these—
It's a system where magic can take flight with ease
Where reality changes and all our requests
And all of our dreams and our goals manifest
Where anything's possible—well within reach—
Even the most unattainable feat
Just a system of cards that's a spiritual tool—
But it's one that can make all your wishes come true

—Dorothy Morrison

4

The Spells

Since the Tarot is constructed of symbols—and symbols speak to all sectors of the brain at once without the benefit of conscious thought—incorporating this system into magical work can bring some very successful results. And keeping that in mind, it would be downright silly not to use the Tarot.

Still, this can present quite a dilemma. Why? Because with Tarot magic, it's necessary to remove certain cards from the deck. In fact, some spells require that you carry particular cards with you for a predetermined amount of time. And even if you can remember to put them back later, this renders your deck useless for anything else—at least temporarily.

If you don't mind not being able to use your deck for a certain length of time, then you're all set—except for one thing. Some spells may require you to do things to your cards that will, for all practical purposes, render them useless forever. You may, for example, have to write on them, fold them, or, even worse, burn them or tear them into bits and flush them down the toilet. And even the staunchest of magical practitioners is going to have some trouble with that.

Fortunately, there is a solution to the problem. Just photocopy the cards you'll need and use these photocopied cards in the the spells when required. Since there's no need to worry about using cards with color, this can be handled without much expense. Place as many cards on the platen as will fit, select the paper size, and press the button. You can cut them apart later.

But what if there isn't a copy shop in close proximity? If you have a scanner, then put it to work and scan the cards. And don't forget to save the files to a disk. That way, you can print the copies yourself, and they'll be handy whenever you need them for spell work.

A Few Reminders . . .

Before you use the Tarot for spellwork, there are a few things you may want to remember. While the Tarot does, indeed, provide its own set of symbols, intent, focus, desire, and concentration are still imperative for successful results. If even one of these factors is missing, the spell will never get off the ground—much less meet its mark in the Cosmos. And this is true for whatever type of magic you choose to perform.

But there's also something else. Something so important, so vital, and so essential to magical success that I can't even begin to stress it enough. Simply put, you have to truly believe that the spell will work. In fact, you have to believe it so soundly that nothing can ever make that faith falter. Not even a little. For if doubt comes creeping in—even just for one fleeting second—all the intent, focus, desire, and concentration in the world isn't going to make things happen.

Sadly enough, most folks don't understand this—or at least, not to the extent that they should. They'll perform a spell one day, then perform another for the same purpose the next. And this sort of behavior is not just time-consuming, it's personal sabotage. Why? Because by performing the second spell without giving the first one time to work, they've just admitted their lack of faith. They've told the Universe that they didn't truly believe that the first effort would meet with success. Otherwise, there wouldn't have been any need to perform the second spell.

For this reason, please don't sabotage yourself. Know that your magic will work, then give it some time to manifest—about three weeks or so. If you haven't gotten the expected results by then, go ahead and try something different. Subscribing to this rule will not just save you time, it will save your nerves as well!

Just one more thing. Remember that the world of magic is—and always will be—governed by the rule of three. This means that everything you do—positive or negative—will come back to you three times. And while you may really enjoy the return on something positive, you may not be able to handle the outcome of an effort that manipulates someone else.

That having been said, here are the spells. Conjure up your faith. Believe in what you're doing. Know that your every effort will meet with success. In doing so, you'll gain that charmed life you thought only possible in your dreams.

Addiction
Addiction Squashing Spell

(*Note:* When performed during the Waning Moon, this spell works well to squelch minor addictions. For major problems, please see a licensed health-care practitioner.)

Materials
The Devil
Death
The Magician

Holding the Devil card in your hands, think about the problems that your addiction is causing and the part that you play in the matter. Visualize yourself being free of the addiction, and say something like:

> *I am no longer a self-saboteur*
> *I am now, instead, a mover and doer*
> *I release myself from the traps I've set*
> *I loose the chains and rip the net*
> *My life moves on, for I am free*
> *As I will so mote it be*

Hold the Death card in your hands and concentrate on starting life anew. See yourself as the person you want to be, completely free of your addiction. Then say something like:

> *Death has come and I'm reborn*
> *From my addiction, I am torn*
> *I am free now—I'm the seed*
> *That sprouts and buds and thrives, indeed*
> *That blossoms freshly where it grows*
> *As I will now, be it so*

Finally, hold the Magician card and see yourself taking complete control of your life. See your reality changing bit by bit, until it becomes the life you wish to lead. Then say:

> *I am the master of my life*
> *I control all stress and strife*
> *I have power—I have strength*
> *And what I come to be at length*
> *Is really truly up to me*
> *As I change my reality*

Place the cards faceup, one on top of the other, with the Magician being the last card (on top). Fold them together into thirds, and carry them with you. When you're free of the addiction, burn them to ash and scatter them on the winds.

Anger

Anger-Releasing Spell

Materials

The Wheel of Fortune

1 small piece of amethyst

Place the stone on top of the card and cover them with your hands. Think about your anger and will it to flow through your fingertips and out of your body. As you feel it leaving your system, chant:

> *Card and stone, I ask of thee*
> *To lift this anger far from me*
> *Grab it, Wheel, as you turn 'round*
> *And twirl it high above the ground*
> *Transforming it into what may*
> *Be used for good upon this day*
> *And once the energy is clear*
> *Ground it in this stone, so dear*

Go outdoors and throw the stone as far as you can, then carry the card with you through the day.

Anger Prevention Charm

Materials

Three of Cups

To curb anger and prevent it from ruining your day, enchant the Three of Cups card by saying something like:

Three of Cups, now hear my plea
Keep anger far away from me
But should it rear its ugly head
Replace the anger then instead
With patience, kindness, and with love
And with your strength I ask you shove
It from my path so all may see
That anger has no hold on me

Carry the card with you constantly.

Anxiety

Anxiety Removal Spell

(*Note:* This spell is designed to aid in the removal of minor panic attacks. For severe cases, please see your health-care practitioner.)

Materials
Nine of Swords
Black wide-tipped marker

Using the marker, draw a large, heavy *X* on the Nine of Swords card. Visualize yourself being happy, lighthearted, and carefree.

Hold the image in your mind, then chant something like:

Anxiety, from me now flee
You are no longer part of me

> *Your power's gone—I have no doubt*
> *I cast you forth and burn you out*

Burn the card to ashes, then flush the ashes down the toilet.

Apathy
Indifference Removal Spell

Materials

The Fool

Holding the Fool card in your hand, visualize the energy of the character depicted flowing into your very core. Then allow it to fill you completely while chanting something like:

> *As the Fool for all to see*
> *Awe and wonder come to me*
> *I am active—I am bold*
> *And as this energy unfolds*
> *Indifference flies away from me*
> *Of its inertia I am free*
> *So I once more can take a stand*
> *Fight for causes, hold a hand*
> *And do my part in what is right*
> *From break of dawn 'til fall of night*

Carry the card with you until all traces of apathy are gone. (This usually takes less than twenty-four hours.)

Charm Against Indifference and Inactivity

Materials
Knight of Swords

Carrying the Knight of Swords card with you on a daily basis chases away indifference and prompts you to take a stand.

Attention
The "Look at Me" Spell

Materials
The World
1 orange candle
Vegetable oil
Allspice
1 small piece of hematite (or a piece
    of hematite jewelry)

To gain the attention of others, perform this spell during the Waxing to Full Moon. Begin by anointing the candle with vegetable oil and rolling it in the allspice. Visualize others seeing you for who you are. Then light the candle, saying something like:

> *As this flame dances in pure light*
> *My image comes forth clear and bright*

Hold the World card in your hand, and, visualizing yourself getting credit for your accomplishments, say:

The World is mine for all to see
For others give it now to me
They give me credit where it's due
Within its warmth, I bask anew

Hold the stone in your hand, while concentrating on others seeing you in a new light and being drawn in your direction. When the stone begins to pulse, say something like:

Little charismatic stone
My magnetism skills now hone
Bring me the pleasure of attention
In a favorable light, let me be mentioned
So all the world, at once shall see
The shining light I've come to be

Place the card in front of the candle and put the stone on top. Leave them there until the candlewick burns out, then carry the stone with you.

Charm to Increase Personal Magnetism

Materials
King of Rods (if you are male)
Queen of Rods (if you are female)

To stand out in a crowd and draw others to you, enchant the appropriate card by saying something like:

King/Queen of Rods, I ask that thee
Bring your radiance now to me

Bring your laughter and your light
Let it shine with all its might
So other folks are drawn to me
As I will so mote it be

Carry the card with you constantly.

Attention Deficit Disorder
Spell to Ease Attention Deficit Disorder

Materials
The Moon
Eight of Swords
Eight of Pentacles
1 small clear quartz crystal

Begin by holding the Moon card in your hand. See yourself being attentive to the things going on around you and say:

At the Moon I cease to bay
I see all that comes my way
Everything, both good and bad
Comes into view now—every tad

Pick up the Eight of Swords, and, using it to cover the previous card, concentrate on seeing things exactly as they are. Say:

Rose-colored glasses aren't for me
For they distort things visually

And as I throw them far away
I see clearly—night and day

Pick up the Eight of Pentacles, and, using it to cover the previous card, visualize yourself acquiring the skills of accelerated concentration and attention span. Say:

Of distractions, I am free
And as they fly away from me
Concentration comes to play
And becomes stronger every day

Still holding all three cards, place the crystal on top and cover it with your other hand. Visualize the powers of concentration and focus streaming into the stone from your third eye, saying:

Stone of power—stone of light
Stone of memory and clear sight
Aid me in these efforts now
Of purest focus and allow
My attention span to grow
And grasp the seeds of knowledge sown

Carry the crystal with you. (*Note:* Continue taking medications prescribed by your health-care practitioner.)

Automobiles

To Prevent Car Malfunction on the Road

Materials

The Chariot

1 tablespoon sage

Charcoal block

Fireproof dish

Begin by placing the Chariot faceup in front of you. Visualize your vehicle running in perfect condition and say:

> *My Chariot, run well and free*
> *As I will so mote it be*

Sprinkle the sage in the center of the card, and visualize all areas of the vehicle functioning perfectly, saying:

> *Sage, protect all moving parts*
> *From malfunction once they start*

Fold the card in half, and then in half again to secure the sage. Lick your finger and draw an invoking pentagram[1] on the packet, saying:

> *By herb and symbol, all is well*
> *And by these words, I seal the spell*
> *Road worthiness is my car's fare*
> *By earth and water, fire and air*

Place the packet on burning charcoal (be sure to burn this in a fireproof dish), and use the smoke to smudge your vehicle.

Protection Against Accidents

Materials

The Chariot

Ace of Swords

Pinch of lavender

Pinch of sage

1 business-size envelope

1 purple candle

Gather your materials during the Waning Moon, and place them in front of the candle. Light the candle and visualize safe journeys in your vehicle. Place your hands on the cards and say:

> *Victory belongs to me*
> *Of accidents I shall be free*
> *Whenever I am in my car*
> *Or drive to places near or far*

Place the cards in the envelope, then add the herbs, saying:

> *A pinch of lavender and sage*
> *Whose power only grows with age*
> *I add now to protect me from*
> *All misfortune that may come*

Seal the envelope and hold it both hands, saying:

> *Cards and herbs, your powers blend*
> *And with their melding, quickly send*

Your protection on its way
In dark of night and light of day

Leave the envelope in front of the candle until the wick burns out, then place it in the glove compartment of your car.

Balance

To Restore Personal Balance Between the Mundane and Spiritual

Materials

The World

Clear adhesive tape

Scissors

Begin by cutting the World card in half horizontally. Then hold one half in each hand, saying something like:

I hold my World in both my hands
To restore my hold on shifting sands
One realm is Spirit—the other is rock
They are both separate, but together I lock
Them into one; for they are both mine

Using the tape to join the card halves, restore the World to its original form. Reinforce the card back with a piece of tape as well. Then say with feeling:

And in them I balance for now and all time

Carry the card with you.

Charm for Mental Balance

Materials

The High Priestess

Holding the card in both hands, enchant it by saying something like:

> *You who float between the planes*
> *Of ether's realm and earthly gains*
> *Bring balance to my mind today*
> *As I live and work and play*
> *So focus will come easily*
> *As I will so mote it be*

Carry the card with you.

Bank Loans

Bank Loan Approval Spell

Materials

Ace of Pentacles

1 green bayberry-scented candle

Candle holder

Green pen or marker

During the New to Full Moon, inscribe a bayberry candle with the amount of cash you need to borrow. Using the green pen, also write that amount across the face of the Ace of Pentacles. Place the candle in its holder, then place the card beneath it. Light the candle and chant something like:

> *By Pentacles and candle fire*
> *Bring to me what I desire*
> *Bring the money that I need*
> *By wing and foot with lightning speed*

Allow the candlewick to burn out, then carry the card in your wallet.

Spell to Receive a Credit Card

Materials
Nine of Pentacles
1 green candle

Begin by lighting the candle, then visualize receiving the credit card in the mail. Fill out the credit card application and place it in front of the candle with the Nine of Pentacles card on top, saying something like:

> *By nine of wishes coming true*
> *Do now what I ask of you*
> *Bring this credit card to me*
> *As I will so mote it be*

Let the candlewick burn out, then lick your finger and use it to draw an invoking pentagram on the face of the application. Mail the application and wait for the card to arrive.

Beauty

General Beauty Spell

Materials

The Star

1 white candle

1 small piece of moonstone

Light the white candle and see the flame melting away all physical flaws. Then hold the Star card in your hands and say something like:

> *Star of wishes—star of light*
> *Star of ethereal beauty, bright*
> *Wrap me with your wondrous awe*
> *So none may see a single flaw*
> *And let the beauty within me*
> *Shine forth for all the world to see*

Put the card in front of the candle and pick up the moonstone, saying something like:

> *Iridescent little stone*
> *Whose beauty often brings a moan*
> *Of delight from humankind*
> *Lend your power—let me shine*
> *Bring your beauty now to me*
> *As I will so mote it be*

Place the stone on top of the card and leave it there until the candlewick burns out. Carry the stone with you.

Spell to See the Beauty in All Situations

Materials

Ace of Cups

1 small piece of unakite

Pinch of soil

Stapler

Holding the Ace of Cups in your hands, enchant the card by saying something like:

> *Ace of Cups, who brings all joy*
> *And beauty to this world, employ*
> *Your powers so that I may see*
> *The wonders now escaping me*
> *Bring them quickly into view*
> *Do now what I ask of you*

Place the stone in the center of the card, then cover it with your hands, saying something like:

> *Stone of pink and green delight*
> *Lend your power and your might*
> *Work with this card that I may see*
> *The beauty hiding now from me*
> *And as it blossoms and unfolds*
> *Revealing secrets that it holds*
> *Let me grasp just what I need*
> *As I plant this little seed*

Sprinkle the soil on top of the stone, then fold the card around it and secure the edges with staples. Carry the packet with you. When you no longer have need for it, bury it in the ground.

Business Success

Online Business Success Spell

Materials

Ace of Pentacles

Page of Rods

Ace of Swords

1 quartz crystal

Take the materials to your computer desk during the New to Full Moon. Then place the cards in a horizontal line on top of the CPU in the following order: Ace of Pentacles, Page of Rods, and Ace of Swords. As you position the cards, say:

> *An Ace for money—a Page for mail*
> *An Ace for victory and all it entails*

Then hold the stone in your dominant hand and say:

> *A stone to magnify business success*
> *And bring positive energy to my request*

Place the stone on top of the Page of Rods and say:

> *Let my modem be busy with commerce and trade*
> *This spell has commenced as this stone is now laid*

Cash Register Charm

Materials

Nine of Pentacles

To increase business in your store, always keep the Nine of Pentacles in the cash register.

Change

Spell to Become Adaptable to Change

Materials

The Wheel of Fortune

To become more adaptable to change and ease its aggravations, just place the Wheel of Fortune card under your pillow. Then before you fall asleep, say:

> *Wheel of Fortune, ease my pain*
> *Bring change swiftly—help me gain*
> *Knowledge as you spin around*
> *Let your blessings, too, abound*
> *So I accept change easily*
> *As I will, so mote it be*

Childbirth

Charm to Ease Childbirth

Materials

The Empress

During the Full Moon before delivery, hold the Empress card in both hands against your abdomen. Then invoke the power of the Mother, saying something like:

> *Mother of all land and sea*
> *Lend your power now to me*
> *Ease the pain of this child's birth*
> *Replace it with your joy and mirth*
> *And hold us safely in your arms*
> *Protecting us from ill and harm*
> *Shield us both—the babe and me*
> *So that this birth comes easily*

Take the card to the birthing room and use it as a focal point during labor.

Clarity

See Things as They Are Spell

Materials

Four of Cups

When clarity of mind is an issue—or you're just having trouble seeing things the way they really are—hold the Four of Cups in your hands to invoke its power and say something like:

> *"What you see is what you get"*
> *Doesn't really seem to fit*
> *Within the situation here*
> *So I ask now: make things clear*
> *Free my mind of clutter now*
> *And in doing so, allow*
> *That knowledge springs from near and far*
> *So I see things just as they are*
> *And grant the answers that I need*
> *Come to me with greatest speed*
> *So I know just what to do*
> *Do, card, what I ask of you*

Carry the card with you.

Clarity of Mind Charm

Materials
Eight of Swords
Black marker

To see situations as they truly are instead of the way you want them to be, draw a large black *X* across the face of the card and say something like:

> *The rose-colored glasses, I toss away*
> *I stop dreaming—now—today*
> *I see things for just what they are*
> *By light of Sun and Moon and Star*
> *All is clear at last for me*
> *As I will so mote it be*

Carry the card with you.

Communication

To Receive a Phone Call or Letter

(*Note:* This spell will not work unless the person in question has your phone number or address!)

Materials
Page of Rods
Adhesive tape

To receive a phone call from someone you haven't heard from in a while, hold the Page of Rods in your hand and visualize yourself totally engrossed in pleasant conversation with the person in question. Once the image is firmly embedded in your mind's eye, say something like:

> *Page of Rods, who heralds all news*
> *Do now what I ask of you*
> *Bring (name of person)'s voice now to my ear*
> *Or let his (her) written words so dear*
> *Grace my presence and my day*
> *Connect me with him (her) right away*

Tape the card to the bottom of your phone or to the inside of your mailbox.

The "Get Your Point Across" Spell

Materials
Page of Rods
1 yellow candle
1 small piece of turquoise

Begin by lighting the candle and seeing your ideas sinking in and meeting with success. Then hold the Page of Rods in your hand, saying something like:

> *Communicative, wordy one*
> *Heed my will and see it done*
> *Let my words ring loud and clear*
> *For all to ponder and to hear*

Hold a piece or turquoise or turquoise jewelry in your hands, and enchant the object by saying something like:

> *Stone of sheer diplomacy*
> *Make my voice heard—let all see*
> *The point that I must make today*
> *And clear all cloudiness away*
> *So that it hits it mark with ease*
> *As I will, so mote it be*

Place the card in front of the candle with the stone on top, and leave it until the candlewick burns out. Carry or wear the stone.

Computers

Basic Protection Charm

Materials
The Magician
Scanner

Scan the Magician card and place it on your hard drive, then use your imaging program to turn it into desktop wallpaper, saying something like:

Magician, act now as a guard
To keep my files from being marred
To keep my data straight and clean
To protect from that which is not seen
To keep viral problems from this space
Keep everything right in its place
Chase all problems far away
Magician, do now what I say

Use the wallpaper for your desktop image.

CPU Protection Spell

Materials

Ace of Pentacles
Ace of Swords
Ace of Rods
Ace of Cups
Adhesive tape

Defragment the hard drive, then turn the computer off. Visualize your system running perfectly day after day. Then tape the Ace of Pentacles card to the top of the CPU and see all the data stored within as being secure and in place. Say something like:

Ace of earth, whose strength endures
All my data, now secure

Tape the Ace of Swords to the bottom of the CPU, and visualize all electronic circuits working flawlessly and connecting one to the other just as they should. Say something like:

> *Ace of Flame, now use your spark*
> *So all connections hit their mark*

Tape the Ace of Rods to the right-hand side of the CPU, while visualizing the fans and cooling system working flawlessly. Say something like:

> *Ace of Winds, with air so cool*
> *Dance within—protect this tool*

Tape the Ace of Cups to the left-hand side of the CPU, and visualize the machine being cleansed of viruses and all other problems. Say something like:

> *Ace of Cups, now chase away*
> *All hazards that would come to play*

Finally, place your hands on the CPU and see a blue light joining the cards both vertically and horizontally, to wrap the CPU in a continual cross. Say something like:

> *Cross of Aces on this tool*
> *Protect by Elemental rule*
> *This machine that's in your care*
> *And shield from problems that would dare*
> *To infiltrate it from without*
> *Or from within or round about*
> *Guard it carefully and well*
> *With these words, I set the spell*

Turn on the computer and know that you'll have no further problems.

Cooperation
Chant for General Cooperation and Teamwork

Materials

The Magician

Hold the Magician card in your hand and think about how he works with the Elements and directs their energies into a flawless blend of cooperative teamwork. Then allow yourself to become the Magician, seeing yourself as the director of the Cosmic flow. Holding the image in your mind's eye, chant:

> *The Magician directs and moves and blends*
> *Elemental energies without end*
> *They work as one in endless motion*
> *A flawless blend without commotion*
> *And as such, it's within my power*
> *To conjure teamwork this very hour*
> *From all who cross my path this day*
> *A seamless blending in every way*
> *Of cooperative efforts for the good of all*
> *Magician aid me—hear my call*

Visualize everyone in your path doing their part and working toward the efforts at hand. Carry the card with you.

Spell for Cooperation at Work

Materials

Three of Rods

Vegetable oil

½ teaspoon cinnamon

½ teaspoon allspice

½ teaspoon clove

1 orange candle

Green pen

With the green pen, begin by drawing a spider web on the Three of Rods to symbolize connectedness, then draw a pentagram on top to represent the magic at hand. Anoint the candle with vegetable oil while visualizing everyone cooperating with each other and handling their workloads pleasantly and efficiently. Roll the candle in the herbs and light the wick, saying something like:

> *Dissension leave and quickly flee*
> *Cooperation is my plea*
> *So all will help and work as one*
> *Until the work's completely done*

Allow the candlewick to burn out, then keep the card hidden somewhere in the workplace. (A drawer in your desk is a good bet.)

Courage

Spell to Summon Courage

Materials

Seven of Rods

1 purple candle

Vegetable oil

Thyme

Begin by anointing the candle with vegetable oil and rolling it in the thyme, while seeing yourself as the most courageous person on the planet. Then light the candle and say something like:

> *I light the flame that burns in me*
> *And from its dance flows bravery*

Then pick up the Seven of Rods card and see yourself meeting all challenges that come your way, no matter how difficult. Know that nothing is beyond your reach, your capacity, or your strength. Feel courage flowing into you in its purest form, pushing out any fears you may have had. Once it has filled you to the brim, hold the card to your third eye, saying something like:

> *Challenges are mine to meet*
> *There are none I can't defeat*
> *And by this card, my courage grows*
> *It fills me from my head to toes*
> *So of timidity, I'm free*
> *As I will so mote it be*

Leave the card in front of the candle until the wick burns out, then carry the card with you.

Courage to be Oneself Charm

Materials
The Hierophant

If you lack the courage to be true to your own individuality, carry the Hierophant card with you. You'll be dancing to you own drummer in no time!

Creativity
Invocation for Creative Flow

Materials
The Magician

Hold the card to your third eye and visualize yourself as being a vessel of creativity, with new ideas constantly flowing through you and into your work. Once you have the image firmly fixed in your mind's eye, invoke the power of the Magician by saying something like:

> *Manipulator—great Magician*
> *On the winds, hear my petition*
> *Lend your great creative power*
> *That I may see this very hour*
> *Innovative ways to mend*
> *The things this day that I must tend*
> *And grant that it will forever flow*
> *Through me as I will it so*

Creativity Charm

Materials
Ace of Rods

To receive a constant flow of creative ideas, enchant the Ace of Rods by saying something like:

> *Ace of creativity*
> *Unlock my mind that I may see*
> *Ideas I haven't seen before*
> *Let them flow right through the door*
> *Keep them coming hard and fast*
> *And as they do, please help me grasp*
> *How to use them cleverly*
> *As I will so mote it be*

Keep the card on your desk or wherever creative flow is necessary.

Depression
Depression Relief Spell

(*Note:* These spells are designed to aid in the relief of minor depression. For severe cases, please see your health-care practitioner.)

Materials
Four of Rods
1 yellow candle
Vegetable oil
1–2 teaspoons thyme

Anoint the candle with vegetable oil, then roll it in the thyme. Light the candle and see all your cares lifting away, and your depression being smothered by happiness. Place the Four of Rods card in front of the candle and cover it with your hands, saying something like:

> *By Four of Rods and happy home*
> *Depression may no longer roam*
> *I smother it with harmony*
> *With happiness, serenity*
> *I call self-love to stamp it out*
> *So it now flees within and out*
> *And suffocates and dies away*
> *It leaves me now—this very day*

Leave the card in place until the candlewick burns out, then carry the card with you.

Depression Relief Charm

Materials
Three of Cups

For immediate relief of depression and its darkness, carry the Three of Cups with you. Use it as a focal point when the blues start to creep in.

Dieting

Spell to Lose Weight

Materials

The Magician

Stand before the mirror on the Waning Moon and hold the Magician card in your dominant hand. Stroke problem areas with the card, while seeing excess pounds disappearing into thin air. With each area, say something like:

> *Controller of the earth and air*
> *And fire and water, hear my prayer*
> *Strike a balance now within*
> *My body—let it start to thin*
> *And let my hunger dissipate*
> *So that I drop this excess weight*
> *But keep me healthy in this task*
> *Until my goal is reached at last*
> *And of further excess, keep me free*
> *As I will so mote it be*

Secure the card to the refrigerator to keep you on the straight and narrow.

Divination

Prophetic Vision Charm

Materials

The High Priestess

Hold the card in your hands and enchant it by saying something like:

> *One who walks between the worlds*
> *And holds the bulk of wisdom's pearls*
> *Whom unseen forces hearken to*
> *Who brings all visions clear and true*
> *Show me what I need to see*
> *As I will so mote it be*

Keep the card with your divination tools.

Divorce

Peaceful Separation Spell

Materials

The Lovers

1 black candle

1 small piece of black onyx

Scissors

During the Waning Moon, light the candle and see all problems coming to a screeching halt. Visualize both parties living happy, separate lives. Then cut the Lovers card in half, separating the characters depicted there.

Place the black onyx in front of the candle, with a card half on either side of the stone. Say something like:

> *Stone that separates the two*
> *Do the work I ask of you*
> *Bring us peace of mind and heart*
> *As our lives anew, we start*
> *And of hassles, make us free*
> *As I will so mote it be*

Leave the arrangement in front of the candle until the wick burns out, then take the card halves and the stone outdoors. Bury the card halves at least a foot apart. Then bury the stone between them, saying something like:

> *Space between us there shall be*
> *Of each other, we are free*
> *Peace between us comes as well*
> *With the grounding of this spell*
> *By power of the Law of Three*
> *As I will so mote it be*

Charm for an Easy Divorce

Materials
The Lovers
Justice
Scissors

Begin by making a vertical cut at the *center top* of the Lovers card. Continue the cut until it ends halfway down the card. Starting at the *center bottom* of the Justice card, make an identical cut. Insert the cut in the Justice card into the cut of the Lovers card to make a four-sided construct. Say something like:

Justice works between us now
Problems it shall disallow
Only what is fair shall pass
Between us as we come at last
To end the life that we once shared
So we may go on unimpaired
To start anew when we are free
As I will so mote it be

Place the object on your dresser or someplace where you'll see it frequently.

Dreams
Prophetic Dream Spell

Materials
The High Priestess
1 purple candle

Light the candle and see yourself dreaming of the future, but resting peacefully. Then hold the High Priestess card in your hands, and say something like:

High Priestess I now call on you
To lift the veil and slip right through
To wander through my dreams this night
And bring the future within sight
Bring forth all that I should see

And make solutions clear to me
Bring forth all that I should know
Clearly marking friend and foe
But bring, too, peaceful rest to me
As I will so mote it be

Place the card in front of the candle and leave it there until the wick burns out. Sleep with the card under your pillow.

Prophetic Dream Charm

Materials
Six of Swords

To receive prophetic dreams and remember them, sleep with the Six of Swords under your pillow.

Eloquence

Spell to Ease the Fear of Public Speaking

Materials
Page of Rods

This spell is very effective when performed before giving presentations or speeches. Just hold the Page of Rods card in your hands and visualize yourself speaking effortlessly with the proper words slipping off your tongue. No stuttering. No hesitation. Nothing but the clear, concise delivery of your ideas. Say something like:

Page of Rods, come now to me
Let my words flow well and free
Squelch the fears with which I'm fraught
Help me to say just what I ought
And let my words ring loud and clear
So all shall understand and hear
Exactly what I have to say
Bring eloquence to me this day

Carry the card with you.

Empathy
Spell to Develop Empathy

Materials
Queen of Cups
1 orange candle

On the night of a Full Moon, light the candle and visualize yourself becoming more empathetic to those around you. See yourself experiencing their emotions and feeling what they feel. Then invoke the power of the Queen of Cups by holding the card in your hands and saying something like:

Queen of Cups who feels the pain
And joy of others without strain
Bring to me these feelings too
That I experience what you do
But as you bring them, this I ask

Let them flow through me, then pass
So within me, they can't stay
Or wreak their havoc with my day

Leave the card in front of the candle until the wick burns out, then place the card under your pillow to do its work while you sleep.

Enemies

Put a Foe on Ice Spell

Materials

Queen or King of your choice
1 zippered plastic bag
Permanent marker
Water

During the Waning to Dark Moon, choose the King or Queen card that most closely resembles your enemy. Using the marker, write the name of the person across the face of the card, then place the card in the plastic bag. Fill the bag half-full of water, press the air out, and zip it shut. Then put the bag in the freezing compartment of your refrigerator, saying something like:

I freeze your power now with ice
I steal it gently without price
You now shall live in icy chill
And cannot touch me with your will
Your power over me is done

And while no harm to you shall come
Of your damage I am free
As I will so mote it be

Do not remove the bag from the freezer, or your enemy will regain power over you.

Fear

Fear Removal Spell

Materials

The Fool

When fear—even unfounded—is a problem for you, hold the Fool card in your hand and visualize yourself being as unconcerned as the character in the picture. Hold the image in your mind's eye and chant something like:

I am not troubled as I skip along
For the Winds wrap around me and whistle a song

Visualize the Winds enveloping you in their care.

The fire of the Sun shines and watches my back

Visualize the Sun ready to burn anyone or anything that means to cause you harm.

The waters of life swirl prepared for attack

Visualize the tides of the Sea standing ready to swallow up anything that makes you afraid.

> *And the earth that I stand on is solid and true*
> *It shields me from danger in all that I do*

Visualize the earth giving you the gift of sure footing as you progress toward your goal. Then chant:

> *With these to defend me, all fears fade away*
> *For the Elements guard me as I work and play*

Carry the card with you for twenty-four hours. Fear will be a thing of the past.

Spell Against Unfounded Fears

Materials
Eight of Cups
Black Marker

When fear is present without rhyme or reason, draw a large black *X* across the face of the Eight of Cups, then crumple it in your hand, saying something like:

> *Fear, be gone—I take your power*
> *Your well-laid plans have now gone sour*
> *I crumple you within my hand*
> *So within me, you can't stand*
> *Your life now wanes for all to see*
> *As I will so mote it be*

Burn the card to ash and scatter it on the winds.

Fertility

Fertility Invocation

Materials

The Empress

Hold the Empress card in your hands and focus on her ability to make everything in her path fertile and pregnant with abundance. Then visualize that power being lent to you in such a way that it fills your every action. (If you wish to become pregnant, also see yourself in the last months of pregnancy.) Once the vision is clear in your mind's eye, invoke the power of the Empress by saying something like:

> *Empress, come now into me*
> *Bless me with fertility*
> *So everything I feel and touch*
> *Grows abundantly as such*
> *Let it blossom—make it thrive*
> *So that it becomes alive*
> *And bears fruit in reality*
> *As I will so mote it be*

Flexibility

Spell to Become More Flexible

Materials

The Moon

1 blue candle

1 small piece of aquamarine

Since the Moon rules Aquarius—and it's the fluid energy of Aquarius that lends power to this spell—this effort works best when the Moon is in that sign. Begin by lighting the candle, and seeing yourself as being flexible, adaptable, and cooperative in all situations. Then place the Moon card in front of the candle and lay the stone on top. Cover the card and stone with your hands and say something like:

> *Aquarius, place of regeneration*
> *Where water flows calmly in pure relaxation*
> *Help me flex—help me flow—in the tide of the sea*
> *Help me grab your life force—make me all I can be*
> *With the help of the moon that shines up in the sky*
> *Bring your magical visions and help me apply*
> *Their mysteries and knowledge to all that I do*
> *Ensure my success as I flow now with you*

Let the candlewick burn out, then carry the stone with you.

Focus

To Restore Balance and Focus to the Mind

Materials

Two of Swords

When you have so much going on in your life that it's hard to focus on any one task, hold the Two of Swords in your hands and think about the chaos surrounding you. Visualize order being restored. See yourself thinking clearly again. See priorities coming to the forefront, and your tasks being handled easily and efficiently. Then chant something like:

> *Disorder, confusion, mixed one with the other*
> *Swords cut away all my mind's endless clutter*
> *With swiftness, I pray, slice away all this mess*
> *Bringing focus and balance once more while I rest*
> *And when I rise, let clear thinking remain*
> *So that all else is gone and priorities reign*

Sleep with the card under your pillow.

Forgiveness

Forgiveness Invocation

Materials

The Sun

During times when forgiveness doesn't come easily, hold the Sun card in your hands and visualize its warming light relieving you of all associated darkness and resentment. Then invoke the spirit of the Sun by saying something like:

> *I am the Sun—I am the light*
> *Who overpowers dark of night*
> *Whose warmth relieves the hurts of old*
> *Whose light within me shines so bold*
> *Whose joy lives here within my core*
> *Whose radiance cannot be ignored*
> *Who brings the power to resolve*
> *All that must now be absolved*
> *And with this power I release*
> *The harm that has destroyed my peace*
> *And forgive what wrong was done*
> *Be it so—I am the Sun*

Freedom
Personal Freedom Spell

Materials

The Hierophant

2 feet of black yarn

Scissors

Wrap the yarn horizontally and vertically around the Hierophant card, then secure the ends with a knot. Say:

> *Bound by society and its expectation*
> *Bound and tied up by ill motivation*

Cut through the yarn with scissors and free the card, saying:

The bonds are now cut and I am now free

Then remove the yarn pieces and flush them down the toilet as you say:

I flush out what I'm not and I keep what is me

Visualize yourself strong and proud, standing up for your beliefs and remaining true to yourself.

Personal Freedom Charm

Materials
The Fool

To obtain the personal freedom that you seek, enchant the Fool card by saying something like:

> *Fool, I call you—make me free*
> *Bring to me the liberty*
> *That I seek once and for all*
> *And grant that my oppressors fall*
> *So never again they shall control*
> *My life and path—Fool, make it so*

Carry the card with you.

Friendship
Spell to Draw New Friends

Materials

Six of Cups

1 pink candle

1 pink envelope (if you only have a white envelope,
    just color it with a pink marker)

1 small piece of gold sunstone

To gain new friends, this spell is best performed during
the Waxing to Full Moon. Begin by lighting the candle
and saying something like:

> *By wick and wax and flame so free*
> *Friends I draw—they run to me*

Then hold the Six of Cups in your hand and visualize
yourself meeting new people, becoming close to them,
and having fun in their company. Say something like:

> *New friends come—they take my hand*
> *We talk and play upon this land*
> *As moths to flame, they come to me*
> *As I will so mote it be*

Place the card—folding it if need be—into the envelope.
Then pick up the stone and say:

> *Sunny stone, shine on my quest*
> *And bring those who will suit me best*
> *Granting they will always be*
> *Truest friends*
> *So mote it be*

Place the stone in the envelope and seal it. Lick your finger and use it to draw an invoking pentagram on the flap. Place it in front of the candle and leave it there until the wick burns out. Carry the envelope with you.

Spell to Keep from Losing Track of Old Friends

Materials

Six of Cups

1 pink candle

Light the candle and hold the Six of Cups card in your dominant hand. Visualize your friends standing in front of you one at a time. Once the image is firmly fixed in your mind, use the card to "draw" a line of connection between you and your friends. Say something like:

> *We are bound by card and cord*
> *Which can't be cut by knife or sword*
> *A strong connection; and as such*
> *We are bound to keep in touch*

Repeat the process with your other friends, then place the card in front of the candle and say something like:

> *Six of Cups, now bind us well*
> *Melting wax, complete the spell*
> *Keep my friends joined unto me*
> *As I will so mote it be*

Leave the card in place until the candlewick burns out.

Gambling

General Gambling Spell

Materials

Seven of Pentacles

1 green candle

A one-dollar bill

½ teaspoon chamomile

On the Waxing to Full Moon, light the candle and see yourself gambling and winning abundantly. Then pick up the Seven of Pentacles and say something like:

> *It's time for harvest—time for gold—*
> *Time for luck and fortune bold*
> *Time for Fate to smile on me*
> *As I will so mote it be*

Place the card facedown in front of the candle, then place the one-dollar bill on top, saying:

> *Money, green and lush, now thrive*
> *Multiply and come alive*
> *By card and cash, this magic's freed*
> *As I will so mote it be*

Sprinkle the chamomile in the center of the one-dollar bill while saying:

> *Be a magnet, chamomile*
> *Draw money to me as lodestones draw steel*
> *Increase my odds and do it fast*
> *Empower the magic that I cast*

Finally, make a parcel out of the card, cash, and herb by folding them together into thirds, into thirds again, and then in half to secure the contents. Say:

> *With card and cash and herb, all three*
> *I cast this spell and set it free*
> *Bring forth cash winnings unto me*
> *As I will so mote it be*

Carry the parcel in your pocket when gambling.

Charm to Increase Gambling Odds

Materials
Nine of Pentacles

To increase gambling luck, just fold the Nine of Pentacles around your paper money before securing it in your money clip or wallet. Carry it with you while gambling.

Gardening
Garden Space Blessing Spell

Materials
Seven of Pentacles
1 cup of water

Stand in the center of your garden space while holding the Seven of Pentacles in both hands. Visualize the garden as planted, growing, thriving, and the fruits of your labor coming to fruition. Then enchant the space by saying something like:

By Elements of earth below
And Sun above and water flow
And wind that dances through the trees
Card of harvest, plant your seeds
I place this space now in your care
To tend all that I shall plant there
And make all flourish fruitfully
As I will so mote it be

Bury the card where you stand, and pour the cup of water on top.

Goals

Goal-Reaching Charm

Materials

Page of Rods

For help in reaching your goals—even those that seem impossible—enchant the Page of Rods card by saying something like:

Page of Rods, now hear my plea
I call now on your expertise
Lend your action—lend your plans
Lay them right into my hands
That I may reach more easily
The goals that are now set for me

Carry the card with you.

Habits

Bad Habits Be Gone Spell

Materials

Death

1 black candle

Fireproof dish

Black pen

Gather your materials during the period of the Waning Moon, and spend some time thinking about the all the bad habits and negative attitudes that stand in your way. As they come to mind, write them across the face of the Death card. Then light the candle and use its flame to set the card on fire. Place it in the fireproof dish and as it burns, say something like:

> *I snuff all life from you this day*
> *Your power wanes and fades away*
> *Until it's gone and you are dead*
> *Leaving only space instead*
> *For all the good life offers me*
> *As I will so mote it be*

When the card is reduced to ash, flush its remains down the toilet. Know that these problems are gone.

Handfasting/Wedding
Spell to Secure a Marriage Proposal

Materials

Two of Cups

1 pink candle

Red permanent marker

Pen or pencil

(*Warning:* While this spell is very effective, it does fall under the manipulative magic category. That being the case, it's important to understand that you, too, will be manipulated by its power—and that's a place you may not want to go.)

On a Friday during the period of the Waxing to Full Moon, color the outside of the candle completely with the red marker. Then, using the pen or pencil, inscribe both of your names on the candle and draw a heart around them.

Light the candle, and, holding the card in your hands, visualize receiving the marriage proposal you desire. Once the image is fixed firmly in the mind's eye, say something like:

> *Intertwining Cups of Two*
> *Do now what I ask of you*
> *Intertwine our hearts as well*
> *And bring the sound of wedding bells*
> *Let my love's heart catch on fire*
> *And bring the words that I desire*

> *So that commitment comes to pass*
> *And we shall take our vows at last*
> *Cups of Two, work fast and well*
> *With these words I cast the spell*

Leave the card in front of the candle until the wick burns out, then place the card beneath your mattress. Sleep in the bed with your love.

Happy Marriage Charm

Materials

Ten of Pentacles

Ten of Cups

Red rosebud or petal

Needle and red thread (or white glue)

On a Sunday during the period of the Waxing to Full Moon, place the Ten of Pentacles in front of you. Visualize all the good things in life coming to both of you. See yourselves as happy, content, and thrilled with the joy of being together. Say something like:

> *Ten of earthly legacy*
> *Let our time together be*
> *Fraught with joy and all the best*
> *Life has to give—and happiness—*
> *All else you now must turn away*
> *And keep it from us night and day*

Place the rosebud in the center of the card and, thinking of your love for each other, say:

> *Like the color of this rose*
> *Our love is deep—it thrives, and grows*
> *Though it ages, it holds fast*
> *This love brings happiness that lasts*

Place the Ten of Cups on top of the rosebud in a horizontal fashion so that it forms a cross with the Ten of Pentacles. See your love for each other growing stronger and stronger; so strong, in fact, that nothing can tear it apart. Say something like:

> *Ten of Cups that reigns above*
> *Bring us everlasting love*
> *Make this marriage strong enough*
> *To conquer spots that may be rough*
> *And fill our hearts with joy so true*
> *That each day together seems brand new*
> *Your blessings on this bond I ask*
> *With these words the spell is cast*

Sew or glue the cross together, securing the rosebud between the cards, while saying something like:

> *Work together cards and flower*
> *Bless this marriage with your power*
> *Do now what I ask of thee*
> *As I will so mote it be*

Hang the charm above the bedroom door.

Harmony

Charm for Harmony in the Home or Workplace

Materials

The Sun

The Moon

Stapler

Place the Moon card facedown, then place the Sun card on top of it, faceup. Staple the two together, securing them on all sides. Visualize all dissension completely evaporating from the atmosphere, and being replaced with peace, serenity, and a sense of cooperation. Say something like:

> *Back to back—as night and day—*
> *Moon and Sun, now come to play*
> *Fill this space with harmony*
> *And let it flow alive and free*
> *Dissolve all tensions from this place*
> *And from it, too, all stress erase*
> *So all shall flow with gentle peace*
> *From this moment and increase*
> *As time goes on—now lend your power*
> *Bring harmony this very hour*

If the problem is at your workplace, place the cards in your desk drawer. Should the problem be at home, however, keep the cards tucked safely into a kitchen drawer or cabinet.

Health/Healing

Healing Chant

Materials

The Star

At dusk, at the first sign of the evening star, hold the Star card in your hands and visualize its light surrounding you, embracing you, and completely enveloping you with its radiance. Then invoke the healing properties of the Star by saying something like:

> *Star of radiance, so bright*
> *Heal my body with your light*
> *Mend my heart and soothe my mind*
> *Throughout me let your magic wind*
> *Through all tissue and all bone*
> *Through all veins where blood does roam*
> *Through all muscles—up the spine*
> *Through the brain, let your light shine*
> *Until it cleanses every spot*
> *Of illness, sickness, and whatnot*
> *And leaves me strengthened with a wealth*
> *Of renewed vitality and good health*
> *Healing Star, I conjure thee*
> *As I will so mote it be*

Heartbreak

Spell to Alleviate Heartbreak

Materials

Three of Swords

Hold the Three of Swords card in your hands and call to mind your misery. Feel it. Cultivate it. Allow it to consume you. (It's okay to scream and cry and throw a fit here. In fact, the more you allow yourself to feel the anger and grief, the deeper the healing will be.) When you've reached the peak of your anguish, throw the card on the floor and stomp on it, then tear it into shreds with as much force as you can muster. Stomp over to the toilet, toss the pieces in, and as you flush the contents, say something like:

> *As water flushes these from view*
> *All hurt is flushed from my life, too*
> *Nevermore to bother me*
> *Of all heartbreak, I am free*
> *And in its place, I find relief*
> *And joy and wonder and belief*
> *That all good things shall come to me*
> *As I will so mote it be*

Take a deep breath, and walk out of the bathroom without looking back.

Heartbreak Prevention Charm

Materials
Page of Swords

To keep from being led down the garden path—the one thing that most often causes broken hearts—enchant the Page of Swords card by saying something like:

> *Card of stealth, I call on thee*
> *To keep deceptions far from me*
> *Show me always what is true*
> *Do now what I ask of you*

Carry the card with you.

Home

Happy Home Spell

Materials
Four of Rods
1 white candle
1 teaspoon dried or powdered thyme

Go to the most centrally located room in your home and light the candle. Place the Four of Rods card in front of the candle and visualize the atmosphere within the home being filled with happiness beyond compare. Then sprinkle the thyme in the center of the card, and fold the edges to secure the herb while saying something like:

Herb of joy and card of home
Bring sheer delight to all who roam
Within this place and down these halls
And grant the space between these walls
Be filled with harmony and bliss
With joy and love and happiness
So wondrous that it touches all:
My friends and guests and those who call
As well as those who live with me
This spell is cast—so mote it be

Leave the packet in front of the candle until the wick burns out, then place the packet under the doormat.

Inspiration

Stream of Inspiration Charm

Materials

Three of Rods

To receive a constant flow of new ideas, enchant the Three of Rods by saying something like:

Three of Rods, creative one
Bring inspiration on the run
Let ideas flow as a stream
A constant flow that picks up steam
Bring them quickly unto me
As I will so mote it be

Keep the card on your desk or in a drawer in your work space.

Jobs

Spell to Find Work Quickly

Materials

Seven of Cups

Eight of Pentacles

1 green candle

Your resume

Light the candle and place your resume in front of it. See yourself working in a job that you love and making a good salary. When the image is firmly fixed in the mind's eye, pick up the Seven of Cups card and say something like:

> *Doors of opportunity*
> *Open quickly unto me*
> *Do not tarry on your way*
> *Fly open for me now—today*

Place the card on top of the resume and pick up the Eight of Pentacles. See yourself learning any skills necessary for the job during your employment. Then say something like:

> *If new skills now I must learn*
> *Bring them to me while I earn*
> *Tarry not, card—hear my plea*
> *Bring a job today for me*

Place the card on top of the Seven of Cups, and leave the stack until the candlewick burns out. Check the want ads, make phone calls, and send out resumes. Carry the cards with you on interviews.

Judgment

Spell for Sound Judgment

Materials

Judgment

1 small clear quartz crystal

If decision-making and sound judgment don't come easy to you, just place a clear quartz crystal on top of the Judgment card. Place your dominant hand on top and say:

> *I listen for my inner voice when good advice I seek*
> *I listen carefully and well*
> *   and heed each word it speaks*
> *I act upon the sound advice*
> *   that comes from deep inside*
> *It is the only voice I hear—I let it override*
> *Suggestions from all other folks,*
> *   for they don't understand*
> *What's right for them is not for me—*
> *   for when I finally stand*
> *To account for what I've done within the life I've had*
> *I'm the one responsible for all deeds good and bad*

Carry the stone with you.

Justice

Plea for Justice Spell

Materials
Seven of Rods
1 bay leaf
1 purple candle
Pen

Begin by writing the problem on the bay leaf and set it aside. (It's not necessary to give a really detailed description here. Just a word or two will do the trick.) Then hold the Seven of Rods card in your hands and see yourself having the courage of conviction necessary to set things straight. Invoke the power of the card by saying something like:

> *Seven of Rods, now hear my call*
> *And aid me toward the good of all*
> *Show me what's wrong—show me what's right*
> *Show me how to win this fight*
> *Stand firm with me to set things straight*
> *Lend strength so I don't hesitate*
> *And grant that justice is well served*
> *So all receive what they deserve*

Then place the bay leaf on top of the card and cover it with your hands, saying something like:

> *Herb of victory and might*
> *Heed my call and ease this plight*

Rectify this easily
As I will so mote it be

Fold the card to secure the bay leaf, and leave it in place until the candlewick burns out. Carry the packet with you until justice is served.

Justice Charm

Materials
Justice
Purple marker

To get a fair shake where legal issues are involved, write your name across the Justice card and carry it with you.

Karmic Debt
Invocation to Ease Karma

Materials
Justice

To keep further Karmic debt from cluttering your life, just hold the Justice card in your hand and say the following chant. It will put you on the way to a debt-free life and help to ease your current Karma.

Justice swing your scales my way
As these Karmic debts I pay
Help me to be just and fair
Help me strive to do my share

So that when this day is done
No more debt shall be tacked on

Liberation
Burden-Releasing Spell

Materials

Ten of Rods

1 white candle

Black permanent marker

Fireproof dish

Using the marker, completely blacken the candle, taking care to color the top and bottom as well. As you color, see all your burdens dissolving into the blackness of oblivion. Then light the candle and say something like:

I've blacked out burdens in my life
I've also blacked out stress and strife
And as I do create this light
They lift and fade far from my sight

Hold the card to the flame to ignite it, then place it in the fireproof dish. As it burns, say something like:

Burdens are no longer mine
They dissolve in record time
And when this card to ash has burned
Liberation shall return

When the ashes have cooled, toss them on the winds.

Love

Perfect Lover Potion

Materials

Ace of Cups

1 cup water

Cup

Saucer

½ teaspoon cinnamon

Honey (optional)

On the Full Moon, heat one cup of water to boiling, and hold the Ace of Cups card in your hands. Visualize meeting your perfect love—since it's imperative that you not put a face on the person, it's best to view him or her from behind—and feel the joy and happiness of true love rising within you. Then place the empty cup on top of the card and say something like:

> *I am the vessel to which true love flows*
> *I hold the seeds from which such love grows*
> *I hold the passion that kindles the fire*
> *I hold the rapture of true love's desire*

Place the cinnamon in the cup and pour the boiling water over it. See the two of you as inseparable, living happily together day to day, and say something like:

> *Herb of both passionate love and desire*
> *Mingle with water brewed hot by the fire*
> *Become now as one to draw true love to me*

> *Become one as we shall—be our destiny*
> *And as you grow stronger with spice and with time*
> *Bring forth the true love to me that is mine*

Cover the cup with a saucer and leave it to steep overnight. Strain out the cinnamon, sweeten with honey, and heat in the microwave if you like. Then drink the tea, saying something like:

> *As I sip this potion, my true love shall be*
> *Drawn like a moth to a flame unto me*
> *Bring now my love by the strength of this tea*
> *As I will now, it shall come to be*

Spell to Keep Romance Alive in a Relationship

Materials
The Lovers
The Sun
The Moon
1 red rosebud

Hold the Sun and Moon cards in your hands on a Friday during the Waxing to Full Moon. Visualize the two of you holding hands and walking beneath the Moon and stars. See yourselves pausing for a kiss and feel the warmth of the Sun filling your hearts with the heat of romance. When the image is fixed firmly in your mind, say something like:

> *Bring back the balance between Moon and Sun*
> *Bring back the enchantment our hearts had once won*

> *Fill both our hearts and our minds with romance*
> *Bring it at once and leave nothing to chance*

Place the cards faceup, with one on top of the other. Then hold the Lovers card in your hands and see yourselves completely smitten with each other, totally lost in the romantic dance you once knew. Say something like:

> *I call on the Lovers and kindle their fire*
> *I call forth the passion of love and desire*
> *I conjure the force of the kiss and the swoon*
> *I conjure it now by the waxing of Moon*

Place the Lovers card on top of the others and pick up the rosebud, saying something like:

> *By bud's heady fragrance and petals of red*
> *I ask that the power of romance be fed*
> *Until it is part of us every day*
> *And beats in our hearts as we live, work, and play*
> *I conjure this both for my partner and me*
> *As I will it now, it forever shall be*

Place the rosebud in the center of the card stack, then fold the stack into thirds as you would a business letter. Place the packet between your box springs and mattress.

Luck

Spell to Change Your Luck

Materials

Ten of Swords

Fireproof dish

Lighter or matches

During the Waning to Dark Moon, hold the Ten of Swords card in your hands and think about everything that's gone wrong in your life. Then mentally fill the card with your angst. Once you've poured every single shred of bad fortune into the card, throw it on the ground and stomp on it, saying something like:

> *I stomp on every shred of grief*
> *That comes my way, for it's the thief*
> *That steals good luck away from me*
> *I seal it here; so mote it be*

Then pick up the card and crumple it in your hand, saying:

> *I crush you now—I take your life*
> *I steal your thunder and your strife*
> *I take your strength and I am free*
> *As I will so mote it be*

Finally, set the card on fire and say something like:

> *All misfortune's burned away*
> *From my life this very day*
> *By card and fire and smoke and ash*

Life starts anew without one dash
Of anything but cheer in sight
I deem it so by flaming light

Flush the ashes down the toilet, and know that good luck is on the way.

Charm for Good Luck in the Home

Materials
The Sun
The World
The Magician
1 horseshoe

Hang the horseshoe above your front door with the points up. Then arrange the cards in a fan with the Magician card in the center. Place the fan inside the "cup" of the horseshoe and secure it, saying something like:

Good luck shall smile on all we do
By fan of fortune in this shoe
Of all else shall this home be free
As I will so mote it be

Lust

Spell to Increase Sexual Performance

Materials

The Lovers

The Devil

1 red candle

1 tablespoon cloves

Red thread

Needle

During the Waxing to Full Moon, light the candle and see you and your partner in the throes of wild, hot, passionate sex. Once the image is fixed firmly in your mind—you should be, at the very least, breathing hard by now—place the Lovers card facedown, and the Devil card faceup on top of it. Holding the cards together, fold them in half with the Devil card facing outside. Stitch two sides together, and place the cloves inside. Then stitch the third side to secure the packet while saying something like:

> *Cards and herb, stir passion's pot*
> *Bring back lust and bring it hot*
> *So when we touch, the sparks shall fly*
> *And blood shall boil until we lie*
> *Satisfied beyond compare*
> *But temper this with loving care*
> *So lust is kept between we two*
> *Do now what I ask of you*

Leave the packet in front of the candle until the wick burns out. Then place the charm either under the bed or between the mattress and box springs.

Magic

Spell to Boost Personal Magic

Materials

The High Priestess

The Magician

1 purple candle

Lock of your hair or a fingernail clipping

Adhesive tape

On the New to Waxing Moon, light the candle and summon your personal power. Feel it rise and swell inside you until it fills you to the brim. Then pick up the High Priestess card and say something like:

> *One who steps between the planes*
> *Of world and spirit, help me gain*
> *The skills to make my magic soar*
> *Right through that heavy Cosmic door*
> *To bring precisely what I ask*
> *High Priestess stand unto this task*

Place the card facedown and pick up the Magician card, saying something like:

> *Manipulator of the air*
> *And fire and sea and earthly fare*

Boost the efforts at my hand
So that they manifest as planned
And grant that I may come to be
A great Magician; hear my plea

Place the card faceup on top of the High Priestess and, holding them together, use the tape to seal three edges of the cards to form a packet. Slip your hair or fingernail clipping inside, saying something like:

Back to back with me betwixt
The power grows until it's fixed
By Magician—Mighty One—
And Priestess of the Moon and Sun
My magic flies to hit its mark
To manifest in light and dark
But harms none on its way to me
As I will so mote it be

Finish sealing the packet with the tape, then leave it in front of the candle until the wick burns out. Keep the charm on the altar when you perform magic.

Menopause

Spell to Ease Menopausal Symptoms

Materials

Nine of Swords

Take the Nine of Swords card into the bathroom and think about the unpleasantness of your symptoms. Pour

all of your misery and distaste into the card, then rip it to
shreds, saying something like:

> *Nine of Swords, I rip you up*
> *Upon you I no longer sup*
> *I rip you right out of my life*
> *I say goodbye to stress and strife*
> *Your day is done—I take control*
> *Reinvention is my goal*
> *And as I toss you far from me*
> *Symptoms ease and cease to be*
> *I take control of what is mine*
> *A happy life that glows and shines*
> *And in that, there's no place for you*
> *Your power's dead and we are through*

Toss the card pieces in the toilet and flush. Your symptoms will begin to ease.

Mental Ability

Charm to Increase Mental Ability

Materials

Two of Swords

Hold the Two of Swords in your hands and visualize
yourself retaining every bit of knowledge—no matter
how miniscule—that's tossed your way. Once the image
is firmly fixed in your mind, enchant the card by saying
something like:

> *Swords of balance and of strength*
> *I call on you to stay at length*
> *To lend your power to my brain*
> *So it absorbs all knowledge gained*
> *And total recall comes to stay*
> *Throughout each busy, hectic day*
> *And grant, too, that it works with ease*
> *So that tough problems will now cease*
> *To confuse or worry me*
> *As I will so mote it be*

Carry the card with you.

Knowledge Retention Charm

Materials
Eight of Pentacles

Hold the Eight of Pentacles card in your hands, and visualize yourself not only retaining every word that you read and every shred of knowledge that comes into your possession, but doing it with ease. Then enchant the card by saying something like:

> *Student's card, O Eight of earth*
> *Fill my head right to its girth*
> *Sort all data—store it well*
> *And in my mind's depths, make it gel*
> *So I can call it forth at will*
> *And keep my memory sharp until*

From this life I am set free
As I will so mote it be

Carry the card with you.

Money
Bill-Paying Spell

Materials

The Empress

1 green candle

Begin by inscribing a green candle with the dollar amount you need. (The Empress abhors greedy folks, so be careful; only request what is necessary.) Place the Empress card in front of the candle and light the wick. Visualize money flowing from the candle flame and spurting forth in all directions. Then chant three times:

Money flow and grow and shine
Empress bring it—make it mine
Bring enough to pay this debt
By these words the spell is set

Let the candlewick burn out, then keep the card with your bills.

Money Jar Spell

Materials

Ace of Pentacles

1 green candle

1 small jar with screw-on lid

1 small piece of aventurine

9 dimes

Cinnamon

Green marker

Gather the materials during the New to Full Moon, then light the candle and visualize money filling your home. Don't stop at allowing it to only cover the floor, though. Keep visualizing until you're standing waist deep in cash. Then roll up the Ace of Pentacles card and place it in the jar, saying something like:

> *Ace of riches and cash flow*
> *Bring me money—make it grow*

Drop the aventurine in the jar, saying something like:

> *Stone that draws all money near*
> *Bring cash unto me right here*

Place the dimes in the jar, one at a time, saying with each placement:

> *Silver twinkle, silver shine*
> *Bring me money—it is mine*

Then sprinkle the contents of the jar with cinnamon, saying something like:

Herb of pure prosperity
Increase my cash flow instantly

Finally, screw the jar lid on tightly and seal it with wax from the candle, then use the marker to draw a dollar bill sign on the lid while saying something like:

Little money-drawing jar
Bring me cash from near and far
Keep it flowing wild and free
As I will so mote it be

Leave the jar in front of the candle until the wick burns out, then store the jar in the back of one of your kitchen cabinets.

Money Draw Charm

Materials

Nine of Pentacles

To ensure that you always have enough money to go around, keep the Nine of Pentacles in your wallet.

Negative Energy
Energy-Neutralizing Spell

Materials

The Sun

1 small piece of black tourmaline

Bowl of water

During the Waning to Dark Moon, place the black tourmaline in a bowl of water. Visualize the stone neutralizing the energy in your home and transforming it into something positive. Put the bowl in a central location in your home, saying something like:

> *Stone that neutralizes all*
> *Hearken to me—hear my call*
> *Go to the root and find the source*
> *Then change this energy's discourse*
> *So negativity is gone*
> *Then blend your power deep and long*
> *Within the water in this bowl*
> *As I will now, make it so*

Then hold the Sun card in your hands and see the energy changing into something even more light, warm, and positive in nature. Say:

> *Warmest Sun, who brings the light*
> *Set this energy now right*
> *Fill this home with warmth and love*
> *Let your light flow from above*

To burn out negativity
As I will so mote it be

Place the card under the bowl and leave it there overnight.
The next day, use the water to asperge the house.

New Endeavors

Spell to Open Oneself to New Endeavors

Materials
Ace of Rods
1 white candle

Light the candle during the New Moon, and watch the
flame dance until you feel its light completely enveloping you. Then hold the Ace of Rods in your hand and
invoke its power by saying something like:

Card of all that's fresh and new
Do now what I ask of you
Bring inspiration, bold and bright
Bring opportunities to light
Bring synchronicity to play
And new beginnings, toss my way
So I may start my life anew
Ace of Rods, I conjure you

Leave the card in front of the candle until the wick burns
out, then carry the card with you.

Nightmares
Charm to Dispel Nightmares

Materials

Six of Swords

1 small piece of citrine

Hold the Six of Swords in your hands and visualize yourself resting peacefully without interruption. See the swords in the card guarding you and scaring away anything that might disturb you. Once the image is firmly fixed in your mind, say something like:

> *Six of Swords, pick up your blades*
> *Protect the place my head is laid*
> *So no nightmare dares to creep*
> *Into the realm of peaceful sleep*
> *So I may rest well through the night*
> *Until the break of morning light*

Put the card down faceup, and, still visualizing the scene, pick up the citrine. Hold the stone until it begins to pulse, then place it against your third eye to attune it to your visualization. Say something like:

> *I call on you, O yellow stone*
> *Absorb all nightmares that may roam*
> *Keep them far away from me*
> *As I will so mote it be*

Place the stone on top of the card and leave it there until it's time to go to bed. Sleep with the stone under your pillow.

Obstacles

Obstacle-Dissolving Spell

Materials

Ace of Swords

Place the card where you can see it, then visualize the sword popping right into your hand. Feel the way it fits in your palm, and spend time getting used to its weight. (This is important because the blade is heavy and double-edged, and if you don't wield it properly, you could hurt yourself.) Then see yourself slicing through stumbling blocks, defending and protecting as foes shy away and enemies fall. Finally, look at the sword and say:

> *Precious sword, champion Ace*
> *What keeps my goals from my embrace*
> *Remove with flawless grace and speed*
> *So my success is sure, indeed*
> *And when I call you to my hand*
> *Come with quickness where'er I stand*

Know that you can call the sword back whenever the need arises.

Obstacle Prevention Charm

Materials

Seven of Rods

To prevent obstacles from blocking your path, enchant the Seven of Rods card by saying something like:

> *Seven of Rods, now hear my plea*
> *Move stumbling blocks away from me*
> *Clear my path of all debris*
> *So that opportunity*
> *Lies solidly in my view*
> *Do now what I ask of you*

Carry the card with you.

Opportunity

Spell to Open the Doors of Opportunity

Materials

Seven of Cups

To open the doors of personal opportunity, stand in a doorway while holding the Seven of Cups card in your hand. See all manner of opportunities coming your way; so many, in fact, that you can't count them on both hands. Then enchant the card by saying something like:

> *Cups of possibility*
> *Quickly cast your light on me*
> *Let all in power see me now*
> *And their favors, please allow*
> *To shower me like golden light*
> *And open doors both left and right*
> *Bringing endless opportunity*
> *As I will so mote it be*

Carry the card with you.

Parking Places

Parking Space Charm

Materials
The High Priestess

Hold the High Priestess card in your hands and visualize her consistently directing you to parking places. When the image is fixed firmly in your mind, say something like:

> *High Priestess, listen—hear my plea*
> *Find a parking space for me*
> *Where'er I travel—near or far—*
> *Within the confines of my car*
> *And point it out that I may see*
> *As I will so mote it be*

Place the card over the visor of you car. Then when you enter a parking lot, remind the High Priestess of her duty by saying something like:

> *High Priestess, I now call on thee*
> *To find a parking place for me*
> *Do your stuff and do it fast*
> *Before another minute's passed*

Find Your Car Charm

Materials

The Chariot

Hold the Chariot card in your hands and see yourself always being able to spot your car in the parking lot. Then enchant the card by saying something like:

> *Chariot, search near and far*
> *Seek and find my waiting car*
> *Bring it quickly into view*
> *Do now what I ask of you*

Carry the card in your purse or wallet. Touch the card when you can't find your car, and it will come into view.

Patience

Patience Chant

Materials

The Fool

Hold the Fool card in your hands and see him on his journey, patiently stopping to listen to those who cross his path and learning from them. Step into the card, take his hand, and say something like:

> *Fool, who journeys hard and long*
> *Whose persistence is so strong*
> *Who endures all paths uphill*
> *That wind and twist and fork at will*

With patience that is unsurpassed
Give to me now what I ask
Lend your gifts that I might learn
To celebrate each twist and turn
Taking time to pluck life's blooms
To smell the rose and its perfume
And lend your patience to me, too
That I may learn now, just as you
Not to hurry on my way
Or rush about through one more day
But wait, instead, for that which comes
As I will, Fool, be it done

Patience Charm

Materials

Temperance

To instill the virtue of patience, enchant the Temperance card by saying something like:

Card of moderation, true
'Tis patience that I ask of you
Bring it gently—let me see
That waiting often is the key
To that which holds life's greatest gifts—
A firmer ground that cannot shift—
And that all shall come to me in time
Bring me patience—make it mine

Carry the card with you.

Peaceful Separation

Parting of the Ways Spell

Materials

The Devil

1 purple candle

1 small piece of black onyx

During the Waning to Dark Moon, light the candle and place the Devil card in front of it. Then watch the candle flame dance for a few moments while holding a small piece of black onyx in your hands. Say:

> *Blackest stone of separation*
> *Bring to me your reparation*
> *Save me from the traps I set*
> *Loose my personal bonds and let*
> *Me climb out of this mess and mire*
> *Give me now what I desire*

Visually fill the stone with your misery, then leave it on top of the card until the candlewick burns out. Bury the stone and card in the ground.

Physical Energy

Charm to Increase Physical Energy

Materials

Knight of Rods

Hold the Knight of Rods card in your hands during the Waxing to Full Moon, and invoke its energy by saying something like:

> *Knight of Rods, now hear my plea*
> *Increase my physical energy*
> *Bring me vigor—bring me speed*
> *Bring the power that I need*
> *To handle all that I must do*
> *Before the Sun sinks out of view*
> *And when I'm done, bring needed rest*
> *So tomorrow, I'll be at my best*

Carry the card with you.

PMS

PMS Relief Charm

Materials

The Empress

Hold the Empress card in your hands and visualize her whisking away all symptoms with a simple wave of her hand. Then enchant the card by saying something like:

> *Empress Mother of us all*
> *Hearken to me—hear my call*
> *Soothe my cramps and ease my bloat*
> *Far from me, this anguish tote*
> *Relieve me now of all distress*
> *And bring an end to PMS*

Carry the card with you.

Problem Solving

Quick Problem-Solving Spell

Materials

Three of Rods

1 yellow candle

Begin by writing your problem on the candle, then light it and say:

> *Candle flame that burns so bright*
> *Bring solutions with your light*

Then, holding the Three of Rods card in your hands, think about the problem at hand. Look at it from every angle, turning it over and over in your mind. Then say something like:

> *Inspiring card of greatest skill*
> *With ideas, my head now fill*
> *Bring solutions—bring them fast*
> *That I may clear this up at last*

Leave the card in front of the candle until the wick burns
out. Carry the card with you until a solution appears.

Solution-Enhancing Spell

Materials

The Emperor

Green pen

Begin this spell by writing all your problems across the
face of the Emperor card. (If you need more room, it's
okay to continue on the back of the card.) Then take the
card outdoors and fold it into a paper airplane. Sail it
through the air as far as you can, and when it lands, say
something like:

> *Emperor, now hear my call*
> *Help solve these problems, one and all*
> *Grant your wisdom; guide my way*
> *Find solutions where they lay*
> *Impart to me your knowledge, so*
> *That I will know which way to go*
> *And once resolved, please chase away*
> *Further problems on this day*

Then bury the plane where it landed, saying something
like:

> *I bury you in solid ground*
> *And by earth's power you are bound*
> *To provide the answers that I need*
> *I conjure you: perform this deed*

Walk away and don't look back. Know that solutions are on their way.

Protection

General Protection Charm

Materials

The High Priestess

Hold the High Priestess card in your hands and visualize the character depicted on the card taking form as a living entity, and growing until she towers over you. Then ask her protection by saying something like:

> *Priestess who hides much from view*
> *I call you forth and conjure you*
> *To protect me from all things that I*
> *Can and can't see with my eyes*
> *Hide me now between the worlds*
> *I ask your power be unfurled*
> *So I am covered with its strength*
> *And hold me in your arms at length*
> *Until this danger passes me*
> *Do now what I ask of thee*

Carry the card with you.

Psychic Development

Chant for Psychic Development

Materials

Strength

The High Priestess

To increase psychism and open its related channels, simply hold the High Priestess and Strength cards to your forehead, then say with feeling:

> *I open psychic channels—*
> *I open psychic ears*
> *I turn the volume up today*
> *So messages are clear*
> *My filters stop the nonsense*
> *That makes me hesitate*
> *I act upon each task today*
> *As it flows on my plate*
> *Each one is handled easily*
> *With promptness and with flair*
> *And as I do, the Universe flows on without a care*

Psychic Attack

Spell to Prevent Psychic Attack in the Home

Materials

Ace of Rods

Ace of Swords

Ace of Cups

Ace of Pentacles

Adhesive tape or pushpins

Compass (optional)

During the Waning to Dark Moon, stand in the center of your home with a compass to determine due east, south, west, and north. Then take the Ace of Rods to the wall portion of your dwelling that faces due east. Visualize a protective barrier at that section extending several feet outside your property boundaries. Once the image is firmly fixed in your mind's eye, say something like:

> *Ace of Rods who rules the east*
> *Secure us from attacks unleashed*
> *By psychic force—protect us all*
> *Ace of air, now heed my call*

Either tape or tack the card to the wall, then proceed to due south with the Ace of Swords. Repeat the prior visualization, and say something like:

> *Ace of Swords, by southern fire*
> *Guard us well from psychic mire*
> *With your flame, protect us all*
> *Ace of fire, now heed my call*

Tape or tack the card to the wall, then proceed to due west with the Ace of Cups. Repeat the visualization and say something like:

> *Ace of Cups who rules the west*
> *Wash away all psychic test*
> *By your tides, protect us all*
> *Ace of water, heed my call*

Tape or tack the card to the wall, then proceed to due north with the Ace of Pentacles. Repeat the visualization and say something like:

> *Fertile Ace who rules the north*
> *Shield us from what may come forth*
> *From psychic attack, protect us all*
> *Ace of earth, now heed my call*

Tape or tack the card to the wall, then proceed to the center of your home. See the barriers of the Elements protecting you and yours from all psychic problems, then say something like:

> *By Elements and Aces four*
> *On psychic crap, I shut the door*
> *So that all live here peacefully*
> *As I will so mote it be*

Leave the cards in place as long as you live in the dwelling.

Charm to Prevent Psychic Attack

Materials
The High Priestess

To ward off the possibility of psychic attack, enchant the High Priestess card by saying something like:

One who walks between the planes
Whom over psychic realms does reign
Please guard me well and watch my back
Protecting me from all attack
And from its backlash, keep me free
As I will so mote it be

Carry the card with you at all times.

Regret
Spell to Wipe Out Regret

Materials
Five of Cups
1 white candle

To alleviate regret, light a white candle and place it behind the Five of Cups. Focus on the flame for a few moments, and visualize the flame burning away all personal regret. When the regret is reduced to ashes in your mind's eye, say:

All regret is burned away
By this dancing flame today

It shall not come again to call
It perishes for once and all

Leave the card in front of the candle until the wick burns out.

Reincarnation
Spell to See Past Lives

Materials
The Hermit

Find a quiet place where you won't be disturbed or interrupted by daily annoyances and aggravations. If that's not possible, then turn off the phone and close the doors and windows. Do whatever it takes to shut out the outside world. The idea here is to have some real peace and quiet. Sit down in a comfortable position and hold the Hermit card in front of you. Say:

Hermit, show me who I am
How I evolved, how my life began
Take me on the journey now
Guide my way and please allow
Me to see what I should know
I'm ready, Hermit! Let us go!

Close your eyes. Inhale. Exhale. Listen to the rhythm of your breathing pattern and the syncopation of your heartbeat. Relax. Then visualize a blank video screen. After a few seconds, pictures will start to move across the screen. Pay attention, for these pictures will clue you in to past lives, show you who you are, and indicate what's in store for you.

Self-Worth

Spell to See Personal Value

Materials

The Hanged One

1 white candle

To boost self-worth, place the Hanged One card beneath a white candle. Light the candle and see its light enveloping you in warmth, love, and joy. Then say the words below with feeling. You'll come away with a whole new attitude. Guaranteed.

> *I am important—I am the light*
> *I am the source that makes the world bright*
> *I am all things as they rise and they ebb*
> *I am an integral strand in the big Cosmic web*

Let the candlewick burn out.

Self-Empowerment Charm

Materials

The World

1 purple candle

Begin by spending a few minutes thinking about the things you've accomplished in your life. Think about what you've learned, the problems you've resolved, and, of course, how wonderful you are. Then light the candle and see yourself going forward with life, meeting with success, and accomplishing more than you've ever dreamed. When the image is fixed firmly in your mind, hold the World card in your hand and say three times:

> *I am successful, for I am the world*
> *I am all goals and solutions unfurled*
> *I am my fate and my destiny*
> *I am the world—I am all I can be*

Leave the card in front of the candle until the wick burns out. Carry the card with you.

Sexual Harassment

Spell to Stop Sexual Harassment

Materials

The Devil

1 black candle

Black permanent marker

Light the candle on a Saturday, and think about your harasser. See all the trouble being caused for you by the person, and feel the anger swell up inside you. Once you've worked yourself up into a state of real fury, grab the Devil card and outline the card margins with the marker, drawing vertical bars through the image like the bars of a cage. Then chant something like:

You're confined by chain and tie
Your actions will no longer fly
You are snared by trap of might
And what you've done now comes to light
So everyone you know shall see
Precisely what you've done to me
I take your strength—I take your will
I take it all except the bill
The heavy cost that you will pay
Beginning on this very day
I conjure now your costly fee
And as I will it, it shall be

Fold the card neatly as many times as is possible and leave it in front of the candle until the wick burns out. If the offender is a work associate, hide the card as close to his or her office as possible. If not, carry the card with you.

Sleep

Anti-Insomnia Spell

Materials
Four of Swords
Black Marker

When insomnia is a problem, draw a big black *X* across the face of the Four of Swords card, dividing it into quarters. Then carefully black out each quarter of the card while chanting something like:

Rest comes easily to me
Of insomnia I am free

When all four quarters are completely colored and the card is completely black, say:

By card and blackest ink, so deep
I gain peaceful, restful sleep

Place the card under your pillow and rest well.

Strength
Obstacle-Removing Affirmation

Materials
Strength

Begin by closing your eyes and clearing your head. Then hold the card in your hand and stand in front of the mirror. Recite the following affirmation. It will give you a firm edge on any obstacles you encounter today.

I am strong and I stand tall
I do not push, but heed the call
Of subtle strength—for it is best
When I am called to stand the test
Brute force shall never lay its claim
To smashing obstacles; the same
Is true of varied opposition
And gaining support for my position
Strength is, instead, the gentle touch
That stands the test of time and such

That brings my foes unto their knees
The subtle strength that's part of me

Stress

Stress Relief Spell

Materials

Ten of Rods

1 white candle

Black permanent marker

To relieve stress, color the outside of a white candle with a black marker. Then place it behind the Ten of Rods and light it, saying:

Burdens, like garbage, I toss far away
Worries go, too—I don't need them today
I simplify life as the excess I clear
'Til I am unburdened—and joy and good cheer
Return to my life and bring back happiness
I cleanse myself of all the muck and the mess

Let the candlewick burn out, then carry the card with you for twenty-four hours.

Simplify My Life Spell

Materials

Temperance

1 black candle

During the period of the Waning Moon, light the candle and think about making your life simpler, getting rid of old baggage and things you don't need. See yourself tossing it all away, turning on your heel, and not looking back. Then hold the card in your hands and say something like:

> *Temperance card of calming peace*
> *Bring moderation now with ease*
> *Help me rifle through my things*
> *And what I don't need, trash and fling*
> *Bring to me a simpler life*
> *Without hassles, stress, or strife*

Leave the card in front of the candle until the wick burns out, then carry it with you until you've finished getting rid of the things you don't need.

Success

Lemonade Success Spell

Materials
The Sun
1 glass of lemonade

Go outside with a glass of lemonade, and place the Sun card beneath it. (If being outside isn't an option, just perform this spell by the nearest window.) Think about all the success and happiness provided by the Sun card. See it filling the glass and infusing the liquid. Then hold the glass high in a toast to the Sun, while saying the following chant. It will go a long way toward removing the things that keep you from getting what you deserve, and help bring about the success that you crave.

> *Sun, who whisks away the night*
> *I drink of your joy and warmth and light*
> *And as I drink, please melt away*
> *Each stumbling block I find today*

Drink the lemonade.

General Success Charm

Materials
The World

To draw small successes to you on a regular basis, enchant the World card by saying something like:

> *I call you, World, to draw success*
> *To bring to me the very best*
> *That life can offer; it is mine*
> *From now until the end of time*
> *Draw it to me—let it flow*
> *As I will it shall be so*

Carry the card with you.

Talents
Hidden Talent Discovery Spell

Materials

Your personal talent card

1 white candle

To discover your hidden talents and make the most of them, begin by locating your personal talent card (see the instructions in chapter 3). Then light the candle and see its light not only guiding you toward these hidden gifts, but showing you how to apply them in your daily life. Hold the card in your hands and study it for a few moments, then say something like:

> *Card of gifts and talents rare*
> *Unto me your meanings bare*
> *Show me what my talents are*
> *And how to use them near and far*
> *To help myself and others, too*
> *Do now what I ask of you*

Continue to study the card through meditation. Ask questions and pay attention to the answers. Carry the card with you on a daily basis, as answers often come when you least expect them.

Theft
To Prevent Theft

Materials
Seven of Swords

Especially helpful if you live in an unsavory neighborhood, this spell is best performed during the Waning Moon. Just hold the Seven of Swords in your hands and rip it in half, saying:

> *By tear of one, I steal your power*
> *Your plans of theft have now gone sour*

Rip it in half again, saying:

> *By tear of two, I seal my home*
> *So that within it you can't roam*

Then rip it in half a third time, saying:

> *By tear of three, all cast their eyes*
> *To strip away your thin disguise*

Finally, burn the pieces to ash, saying:

> *I cast a light on you with fire*
> *So all shall see what you desire*

I burn your greed to ash this day
Protecting all who pass your way

Flush the ashes down the toilet.

Spell to Locate Stolen Objects

Materials
The High Priestess
Page of Swords

Once you've filed a police report—this is important in the scheme of things—use this spell to speed the return of your belongings. Hold the High Priestess card in your hands and see her throwing back the veil to reveal the missing objects, saying something like:

Keeper of the light and dark
I ask you now to find and mark
The missing objects that are mine
Shed your light and let them shine

Then cover the High Priestess with the Page of Swords. Visualize him cutting through any deceit during the questioning of potential suspects. (Please don't skip this part, for you don't want any innocent party charged with the crime at hand!) Say:

Page of Swords, cut through deceit
And make this task an easy feat
So that the thief is put away
And none else for his (her) crimes shall pay

Place the cards under the phone.

Time

Time-Freezing Spell

Materials

The Wheel of Fortune

To stop time temporarily, hold the Wheel of Fortune card in your hands and see the wheel stopping without further movement. As it stops, visualize all time standing still. (This takes a great deal of concentration!) Then finalize the spell by saying something like:

> *Wheel of Fortune, stop your turns*
> *So not another second burns*
> *Stop all time and keep it still*
> *Do now, Wheel, just as I will*

Use the visualization whenever you are running late or need an extra few minutes of uninterrupted time to complete a project.

Traffic

Charm to Ease Traffic Flow

Materials

The Chariot

2 feet of ¼" yellow ribbon

Single hole punch

1 yellow candle

On the New to Full Moon, gather the materials and light the yellow candle. Watch the flame burn higher and higher, while visualizing traffic flowing smoothly without stoppage from accidents or other problems. Then pick up the Chariot card and, continuing the visualization, say something like:

> *Chariot of speed and light*
> *I conjure forth your strength and might*
> *To ease all traffic flow where I*
> *May choose to travel, day or night*
> *And keep all harm away from me*
> *As I will so mote it be*

Punch a hole in the top of the card and thread the ribbon through, tying the ends together. Leave the card in front of the candle until the wick burns out. Hang the charm over the rearview mirror of your vehicle.

Travel
Safe Travel Charm

Materials
The Chariot
Aluminum foil

Holding the Chariot card in your hands, visualize all who ride in your vehicle being safe from harm and enjoying pleasant journeys. Then wrap the card in aluminum foil with the shiny side facing out, while seeing any potential danger bouncing away from the vehicle and its occupants. Say something like:

Shield all passengers in this car
Where'er they travel, near or far
From harm or danger that may wait
For from this moment, it's your fate
To bounce all problems far away
And keep all safe here night and day

Place the packet in the glove box.

Luggage Arrival Spell

Materials
The Chariot
Pinch of lavender
White glue

To ensure that luggage arrives with you when traveling, place the lavender on top of the card. Fold the card in thirds, and then in thirds again. Secure the parcel with a bit of glue, saying something like:

Herb and Chariot affix
Unto this bag—protect from tricks
From schedule changes and travel woes
Make sure it goes just where I go
Without one single reservation
So it meets me at my destination

Place the parcel in your bag. (If you have additional bags, make one parcel for each.)

Truth

Uncover the Truth Spell

Materials

Page of Swords

1 small clear quartz crystal

When cutting through deception is an issue, hold the small clear quartz crystal to your third eye and spend a few minutes concentrating on the circumstances and the people involved. Then place the stone on top of the Page of Swords, cover it with your dominant hand, and say something like:

> *Stone of knowledge amplified*
> *By Page of Swords, you cannot lie*
> *Find the truth and then allow*
> *Me to see it—bring it now*

Leave them in place. Just before you go to bed, remove the stone, hold it to your third eye, and watch as the vision unfolds.

Unwanted Guests

Spell to Deter Unwanted Guests

Materials

The Devil

Patchouli oil

On the Waning to Dark Moon, dip your index finger in patchouli oil and use it to draw a banishing pentagram[2] on the face of the Devil card. Visualize all unwanted guests not only being banished from your home, but refusing to set foot on your property. Then bury the card near your front door while saying something like:

> *Patchouli leads you far from here*
> *You may not even come as near*
> *As the gate that seals my land*
> *For all and ever, you are banned*
> *All bonds are gone 'twixt you and me*
> *As I will so mote it be*

Victory
Spell for General Victory

Materials

Ace of Swords

1 bay leaf

1 yellow candle

Charcoal block

Fireproof dish

On a Sunday or Thursday during the Waxing Moon, light the candle and see all your efforts meeting with success. Then pick up the Ace of Swords card, saying something like:

> *I hold the sword of victory*
> *I hold it now for all to see*
> *It is mine in all I do*

> *And works its magic through and through*
> *So all endeavors that are mine*
> *Meet with victory's radiant shine*

Place the card on top of the burning charcoal (be sure to burn this in a fireproof dish), then add the bay leaf, saying:

> *By card and herb in flame of fire*
> *Bring me now what I desire*
> *Bring sweet victory unto me*
> *As I will so mote it be*

Let the candlewick burn out, then bury any leftover wax and ashes in the ground.

Charm to Prevent Defeat

Materials
Six of Rods

To keep personal missions from meeting with defeat, enchant the Six of Rods card by saying something like:

> *Bring victories and make them sweet*
> *For I shall not accept defeat*
> *Six of Rods, now hear my plea*
> *Bring them swiftly unto me*

Carry the card with you.

War

Spell to Prevent War

Materials

Ace of Rods

Ace of Swords

Ace of Cups

Ace of Pentacles

The Magician

1 purple candle

A symbol of the land you wish to protect
(this may be a small flag, a picture, or
any other meaningful symbol)

During the Waning to Dark Moon, light the candle and hold the Ace of Rods card in your hands while visualizing gale force winds blowing any would-be attackers far away. Say something like:

> *Ace of Rods, blow forth your wind*
> *And with its force, attacks now send*
> *Coursing far away from here*
> *And from the country I hold dear*

Put the card in front of the candle and pick up the Ace of Swords. See its blade holding all who wish to wage war at bay. Say something like:

> *Ace of Swords, now wield your blade*
> *Until all harm and danger fades*
> *Protect us well and hold at bay*
> *All attacks that come this way*

Place the card on top of the Ace of Rods. Then pick up the Ace of Cups, and visualize all who wish to do harm being washed away by the tides of the sea. Say something like:

> *Ace of Cups who holds life's source*
> *Wash out all attacking force*
> *Drown out those who would wage war*
> *And keep them from shores near and far*

Place the card on top of the Ace of Swords. Then pick up the Ace of Pentacles and see the attackers being unable to penetrate the country. Say something like:

> *Ace of Pentacles and earth*
> *Protect this land and shield her girth*
> *By swamp and rock and shifting sand*
> *Give them no sure place to stand*

Place the card on top of the Ace of Cups. Then pick up the Magician card and invoke its aid by seeing the character depicted in the card whisking away all impending attacks with the wave of a hand. Say something like:

> *And Magician, lend your aid*
> *Stand as strong as steel-wrought blade*
> *Work the power of the wind*
> *And tide of sea that you may send*
> *All harm away now from the earth*
> *So we may live in love and mirth*
> *And of attacks we may be free*
> *Do now what I ask of thee*

Place the symbol on top of the cards and leave it there until the candlewick burns out. Fold the cards around the symbol and store it close to your altar or magical work area.

Spell To Protect a Soldier Going to War

Materials

The Empress

The Emperor

1 white candle

Photograph of the soldier

Picture frame

Light the candle and place the photograph in front of it. Look at the photo and visualize a white light of protection completely enveloping the person depicted in the picture. See that person as coming through the war safely. Then pick up the Empress Card and say something like:

> *Loving Mother of us all*
> *Protect this soldier from a fall*
> *Hold him (her) in your warm embrace*
> *And shield him (her) as he (she) takes his (her) place*
> *Within this chaos that's called war*
> *Protect him (her) high, low, near, and far*
> *And bring him (her) safely back to me*
> *As I will so mote it be*

Place the card on the left side of the photo, and pick up the Emperor card. See the Emperor giving the soldier wise counsel, and guiding him or her through tough decisions. Say something like:

Father, I now call on thee
To guide this soldier constantly
Through all that tossed into his (her) way
And lend your wisdom every day
So that decisions will be clear
Protect against both harm and fear
Then grant safe passage back to me
As I will so mote it be

Put the card on the right side of the photo, and leave in place until the candlewick burns out. Tape the cards side by side to the back of the photo, and place in the picture frame.

Weather

Spell to Change the Weather

Materials

Ace of Pentacles
Ace of Rods
Ace of Cups
Ace of Swords

Using the Ace of Pentacles to represent the spot where a change of weather is necessary, place the card in front of you. Then hold the other three Aces in your hands and say something like:

> *Elements, I conjure thee*
> *To do my will now—hear my plea*
> *Change the weather as I ask*
> *Hearken quickly to this task*

The next step depends on what sort of weather you're conjuring. If it's rain, place the Ace of Cups over the Ace of Pentacles and say something like:

> *Ace of Cups, now bring the rain*
> *Soothe this space's cracked, dry pain*
> *Cleanse it so of drought we're free*
> *As I will, so mote it be*

To dry the rain with wind, cover the Ace of Pentacles with the Ace of Rods and say something like:

> *Ace of Rods and gentle breeze*
> *Dance now through both bush and tree*
> *Dry this space of flooding woe*
> *As I will, it shall be so*

For warmth and sunshine, place the Ace of Swords on top and say something like:

> *Ace of Swords that brings the Sun*
> *Lend your warmth 'til day is done*
> *Bring the sunshine now to me*
> *As I will, so mote it be*

Leave the cards in place until the weather changes appropriately.

Wisdom

Wise Decision Spell

Materials

The Emperor

1 purple candle

1 envelope or small cloth bag

1 teaspoon sage

Especially effective when decision-making doesn't come easily, this spell is best performed on the Full Moon. Simply light the candle, then hold the Emperor card in both hands and visualize yourself making sound decisions. Say something like:

> *Emperor, upon the throne*
> *The skills of wisdom, now please hone*
> *And entreat them unto me*
> *As I will so mote it be*

Place the card in the envelope or bag, then sprinkle the sage inside, saying:

> *Herb of wisdom, lend your power*
> *Unto my spell this very hour*
> *And grant that I may find with ease*
> *A solution without Karmic fees*

Seal the envelope (or close the bag) and place it in front of the candle, saying:

> *Herb and card, become a charm*
> *Powerful, but without harm*
> *That grants pure wisdom unto me*
> *As I will so mote it be*

Leave the parcel there until the candlewick burns out, then place it on your headboard or under your pillow.

Wishes

Crystal Wish Spell

Materials

The Star

1 green candle

1 small clear quartz crystal

Begin by inscribing your wishes on a green candle. (Make sure to be specific; the Universe has no sense of reason, and will only provide what you request.) Place the Star card in front of the candle and lay a quartz crystal on top. Then light the candle and ask the Star's help by saying:

> *Star of wonder, Star of light*
> *Star of wishes burning bright*
> *In your light, my wishes bask*
> *Bring to me just what I ask*

As the candle burns, spend a few moments in visualization mode. See your dreams coming true, and watch as they manifest in vivid detail. Let the candlewick burn out, then place the card and stone under your pillow. Leave them there for seven days.

Bay Leaf Wish Spell

Materials
Nine of Cups
Marking pen in a color appropriate to your wish
1 bay leaf
Charcoal block
Fireproof dish

During the Waxing to Full Moon, use the marking pen to write your wish on the face of the Nine of Cups. Place the bay leaf on top, and fold the edges of the card to secure the herb. Burn the packet to ash on charcoal (be sure to burn this in a fireproof dish) while visualizing your wish coming to fruition. When the ashes cool, bury them in the ground.

Endnotes

1. To draw an invoking pentagram, start at the top point, move down toward the bottom left-hand corner, up to the right-hand point, over to the left-hand point, down to the bottom right-hand corner, and back up to the top point for completion.

2. A banishing pentagram is drawn from the top point to the lower right-hand corner, up to the left-hand center corner, over to the right-hand center corner, down to the left-hand lower corner, and back up to the top corner for completion.

Invoking Pentagram

Banishing Pentagram

Afterword

Creative effort—the willingness to personalize, improvise, and act on inspiration—is important to magic. Why? Because creativity is the matrix from which all magic flows. It's the catalyst that gets it off the ground, sends it to the Universe, and brings it back, forever changed into the manifestation of our desires. Without it, magic would simply cease to exist.

This is not to say that the spells in this book won't work for you as written. They will. However, you may feel the need to change them somewhat to suit your own purposes. And that being the case, it's perfectly fine to add something here, subtract something there, or maybe even substitute one thing for another. Worried that you'll screw things up? Don't be. Just use the components listed in the appendices that follow. They're guaranteed to keep your magic flowing flawlessly and bring about the results you desire.

Appendix A

The Magical Uses of Herbs, Plants, and Flowers

Anger Management: almond, catnip, chamomile, elecampane, rose, lemon balm, lavender, mint, passion flower, vervain

Anxiety Management: skullcap, valerian

Apathy: ginger, peppermint

Beauty: avocado, catnip, flax, ginseng, maidenhair fern, rose, rosemary, witch hazel

Business Success: basil, hawthorn, sandalwood, squill root

Courage: borage, cedar, columbine, masterwort, mullein, sweet pea, thyme, tonka bean, yarrow

Depression Management: catnip, celandine, daisy, hawthorn, honeysuckle, hyacinth, lemon balm, lily of the valley, marjoram, saffron, shepherd's purse

Divination: camphor, dandelion, goldenrod, ground ivy, henbane, hazelnut, hibiscus, meadowsweet, mugwort, pomegranate

Employment: bergamot, bayberry, bay leaf, pecan, pine

Enemies: patchouli, slippery elm

Friendship: lemon, orange, sunflower, sweet pea, tonka bean, vanilla

Gambling: buckeye, chamomile, pine

Health/Healing: allspice, apple, barley, bay leaf, blackberry, cedar, cinnamon, comfrey, elder, eucalyptus, fennel, flax, garlic, ginseng, goldenseal, heliotrope, hops, horehound, ivy, lemon balm, life everlasting, mint, mugwort, myrrh, nasturtium, nutmeg, oak, olive, onion, peppermint, persimmon, pine, plantain, rosemary, rowan, rue, saffron, sandalwood, shepherd's purse, thistle, thyme, vervain, violet, willow, wintergreen, yerba santa

Heartbreak Management: apple, bittersweet, cyclamen, honeysuckle, jasmine, lemon balm, magnolia, peach, strawberry, yarrow

Legal Matters: buckthorn, celandine, chamomile, galangal, hickory, High John, marigold

Liberation: chicory, cypress, lavender, lotus, mistletoe, moon flower

Love: Adam-and-Eve root, allspice, apple, apricot, balm of Gilead, basil, bleeding heart, cardamom, catnip, chamomile, cinnamon, clove, columbine, copal, coriander, crocus, cubeb, daffodil, daisy, damiana, dill, elecampane, elm, endive, fig, gardenia, geranium, ginger, ginseng, hibiscus, hyacinth, Indian paintbrush, jasmine, juniper, kava-kava, lady's mantle,

lavender, lemon balm, lemon verbena, linden,
lobelia, lotus, loveage, maidenhair fern, mandrake,
maple, marjoram, myrtle, nutmeg, orchid, pansy,
peach, peppermint, periwinkle, poppy, primrose,
rose, rosemary, rue, saffron, skullcap, spearmint,
spiderwort, strawberry, thyme, tonka bean, tulip,
vanilla, vervain, violet, willow, wood betony, yarrow

Luck: allspice, anise, bluebell, calamus, china berry,
daffodil, hazel, heather, holly, Job's tears, linden,
lucky hand, nutmeg, oak, orange, persimmon,
pomegranate, poppy, rose, snakeroot, vetivert, violet

Lust: allspice, caraway, carrot, cattail, cinnamon,
cinquefoil, clove, damiana, deerstongue, dill,
foxglove, galangal, ginseng, hibiscus, mistletoe,
parsley, rosemary, sesame, southernwood, vanilla,
violet, yohimbe

Menopause: black cohosh, lavender, peppermint, sage

Mental Powers: all-heal, bay leaf, caraway, celery seed,
forget-me-not, hazel, horehound, lily of the valley,
lotus, pansy, periwinkle, rue, sandalwood, spikenard,
summer savory, spearmint

Nightmare Prevention: mullein, chamomile

PMS: feverfew, jasmine, lavender, rose

Prophetic Dreams: anise, chamomile, cinquefoil, cloves,
heliotrope, jasmine, mimosa, mint, mugwort, rose,
rosemary, valerian

Prosperity: almond, bay leaf, basil, bergamot, cedar,
chamomile, cinnamon, cinquefoil, clover, mandrake,

marjoram, may apple, myrtle, oak, orange mint,
parsley, pecan, pine, snapdragon, sunflower, sweet
woodruff, tonka bean, tulip, vanilla, vervain, wheat

Protection: African violet, agrimony, aloe vera, alyssum,
angelica, anise, arrowroot, asafoetida, balm of Gilead,
basil, bay leaf, birch, bladder wrack, boneset,
bromeliad, broom, burdock, cactus, calamus,
caraway, carnation, cedar, chrysanthemum,
cinnamon, cinquefoil, clove, clover, cumin, curry,
cyclamen, cypress, datura, dill, dogwood, dragon's
blood, elder, elecampane, eucalyptus, fennel,
feverwort, flax, fleabane, foxglove, frankincense,
galangal, garlic, geranium, ginseng, heather, holly,
honeysuckle, horehound, houseleek, hyacinth,
hyssop, ivy, juniper, lady's slipper, larkspur, lavender,
lilac, lily, linden, lotus, lucky hand, mallow,
mandrake, marigold, mimosa, mint, mistletoe,
mugwort, mulberry, mullein, mustard, myrrh, nettle,
oak, olive, onion, parsley, pennyroyal, peony, pepper,
periwinkle, pine, plantain, primrose, quince, radish,
raspberry, rattlesnake root, rhubarb, rose, rowan,
rue, sage, St. John's wort, sandalwood, snapdragon,
southernwood, Spanish moss, sweet woodruff,
thistle, tulip, valerian, vervain, violet, willow,
wintergreen, witch hazel, wolfsbane, wormwood,
wood betony, yucca

Psychic Ability: celery, cinnamon, citronella, elecampane, eyebright, flax, galangal, honeysuckle,
lemongrass, mace, marigold, mugwort, peppermint,

rose, rowan, star anise, thyme, uva ursa, wormwood, yarrow

Sexual Harassment Management: bergamot, camphor, salt petre, vervain, witch hazel

Sleep: agrimony, chamomile, cinquefoil, elder, hops, lavender, linden, peppermint, rosemary, shepherd's purse, thyme, valerian, vervain

Strength: acorn, bay leaf, carnation, mugwort, mulberry, pennyroyal, plantain, St. John's wort, thistle

Stress Management: calendula, chamomile, comfrey, hops, lavender, nettle, oats, passion flower, St. John's wort, skullcap

Success: cinnamon, clover, ginger, High John, lemon balm, orange, rowan

Theft: caraway, elder, garlic, gentian, juniper, rosemary, vetivert

Travel: bladder wrack, lavender

Victory: bay leaf, High John, olive

Wisdom: hazel, rowan, sage, spikenard

Wishes: bay leaf, dandelion, dogwood, hazel, Job's tears, sage, sunflower, tonka bean, vanilla, vervain, violet, walnut

Appendix B

The Magical Uses of Stones

Anger Management: amethyst, carnelian, lepidolite, topaz

Beauty: amber, cat's-eye, jasper, opal, rose quartz, unakite

Business Success: green agate, aventurine, bloodstone, emerald, jade, lapis lazuli, malachite, green tourmaline

Change: ametrine, opal, unakite, watermelon tourmaline

Childbirth: geode, moonstone, mother-of-pearl

Courage: agate, amethyst, aquamarine, amethyst, bloodstone, carnelian, diamond, hematite, lapis lazuli, tiger-eye, watermelon tourmaline, turquoise

Creativity: orange calcite, citrine, opal, topaz

Depression Management: blue agate, kunzite

Dieting: moonstone, blue topaz

Divination: hematite, moonstone, rainbow obsidian, opal, quartz crystal

Dreams: amethyst, azurite, citrine, opal, snowflake obsidian

Eloquence: carnelian, celestite, emerald

Friendship: chrysoprase, rose quartz, pink tourmaline, turquoise

Gambling: amazonite, aventurine, tiger-eye

Gardening: green agate, moss agate, jade, malachite, quartz crystal

Bad Habit Management: moonstone, obsidian, black onyx

Healing/Health: green agate, banded agate, amethyst, aventurine, azurite, bloodstone, carnelian, chrysoprase, coral, diamond, peridot, petrified wood, quartz crystal, smoky quartz, sapphire, sodalite, staurolite, sugilite, sunstone, yellow topaz, turquoise

Love: alexandrite, amber, amethyst, chrysocolla, diamond, emerald, jade, lapis lazuli, lepidolite, malachite, moonstone, opal, pearl, rose quartz, rhodocrosite, sapphire, topaz, pink tourmaline, turquoise

Luck: alexandrite, amber, Apache tear, aventurine, chalcedony, chrysoprase, holey stones, lepidolite, opal, pearl, tiger-eye, turquoise

Lust: carnelian, coral, sunstone, mahogany obsidian

Magical Power: bloodstone, holey stones, quartz crystal, malachite, opal, ruby

Mental Ability: aventurine, citrine, emerald, fluorite, quartz crystal

Nightmare Prevention: chalcedony, citrine, holey stones, lepidolite, ruby

Peaceful Separation: black onyx, black tourmaline

Physical Energy: banded agate, garnet, quartz crystal, rhodocrosite, sunstone, tiger-eye

Prosperity: abalone, green agate, aventurine, bloodstone, chyrsoprase, emerald, jade, mother-of-pearl, malachite, opal, pearl, peridot, ruby, sapphire, staurolite, tiger-eye, green tourmaline

Protection: apache tear, carnelian, chalcedony, chrysoprase, citrine, coral, diamond, emerald, flint, garnet, holey stones, jade, jasper, lapis lazuli, lepidolite, malachite, marble, moonstone, mother-of-pearl, obsidian pearl, peridot, petrified wood, quartz crystal, ruby, salt, staurolite, sunstone, tiger-eye, smoky topaz, black tourmaline, turquoise

Psychic Ability: amethyst, aquamarine, azurite, citrine, quartz crystal, emerald, holey stones, lapis lazuli

Psychic Attack Management: alexandrite, fluorite, hematite, opal

Stress Management: amethyst, chyrsoprase, leopard skin agate, jade, brecciated jasper, paua shell

Success: amazonite, chrysoprase, marble, sunstone

Theft Management: garnet, cubic zirconia

Travel: aquamarine, chalcedony

Wisdom: amethyst, chrysocolla, coral, jade, sodalite, sugilite

Appendix C

Candle Color Substitutions and Magical Uses

Black: break bad habits, Crone aspect of the Triple Goddess, stop gossip, separation, uncovering truth, wisdom

Pale Blue: calmness, clarify, healing, peace, pleasant dreams, tranquility

Dark Blue: feminine deities, organization, water element

Brown: grounding, diffusing potentially harmful situations, relieve excess energy

Gold: financial increase, personal security, solar deities, the God

Green: earth element, fertility, growth, healing, independence, obstacles, productivity, prosperity

Lavender: stress and tension relief, knowledge retention, inner beauty, mental ability

Mauve: cooperation, intuitive power, psychic ability, self-confidence, self-trust

Orange: attraction, business projects, business proposals, indifference, personal motivation, productivity, study

Peach: empathy, friendship, kindness, sympathy

Pink: friendship, harmony, love, romance, self-love

Purple: akasha element, job interviews, mental power, psychic power, protection, respect, spirituality, victory

Red: control, fire element, lust, Mother aspect of the Triple Goddess, passion, physical energy, physical strength, sexual desire, timidity

Silver: lunar deities, peace, serenity, the Goddess

Teal: agricultural efforts, balance, self-control, decision-making, practical matters, trust

Turquoise: diplomacy, eloquence, knowledge retention, logic, love, relaxation, stress relief, study

White: clarity, focus, Maiden aspect of the Triple Goddess, protection, substitution for any other color, spiritual guidance, tension relief

Yellow: air element, communication, creative endeavors, joy, success

Appendix D

Reading Spreads

Spread One: Past, Present, Future

Past	1	2	3
Present	4	5	6
Future	7	8	9

Spread Two: Celtic Cross

Final Outcome

10

Immediate Future

4

**Querent's
Hopes & Fears**

9

Past

5

**Current
Situation**

1

**Distant
Future**

6

2
Crossing

**How Others View
the Querent**

8

Underlying Circumstances

3

The Querent

7

Spread Three: Clarification

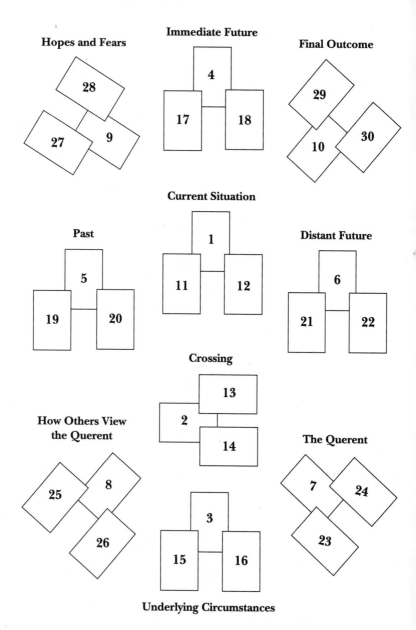

Hopes and Fears

28
27 9

Immediate Future

4
17 18

Final Outcome

29
10 30

Current Situation

1
11 12

Past

5
19 20

Distant Future

6
21 22

Crossing

13
2
14

How Others View the Querent

25 8
26

The Querent

7 24
23

Underlying Circumstances

3
15 16

Bibliography

Abadie, M. J. *The Everything Tarot Book*. Holbrook, Mass.: Adams Media Corporation, 1999.

Beyerl, Paul. *Master Book of Herbalism*. Custer, Wash.: Phoenix Publishing, 1984.

Clarson, Laura G. *Tarot Unveiled: The Method To Its Magic*. Stamford, Conn.: U.S. Games Systems, Inc., 1984.

Connolly, Eileen. *Tarot: A New Handbook for the Apprentice*. North Hollywood, Calif: Newcastle Publishing, Inc., 1979.

Cunningham, Scott. *Cunningham's Encyclopedia of Crystal, Gem and Metal Magic*. St. Paul, Minn.: Llewellyn Publications, 1987.

———. *Cunningham's Encyclopedia of Magical Herbs*. St. Paul, Minn.: Llewellyn Publications, 1986.

David, Judithann H., Ph.D. *Michael's Gemstone Dictionary*. Channeled by J. P. Van Hulle. Orinda, Calif.: The Michael Educational Foundation and Affinity Press, 1986.

Galenorn, Yasmine. *Tarot Journeys*. St. Paul, Minn.: Llewellyn Publications, 1999.

Greer, Mary K. *Tarot for Your Self*. North Hollywood, Calif.: Newcastle Publishing, Inc., 1984.

Jette, Christine. *Tarot for the Healing Heart*. St. Paul, Minn.: Llewellyn Publications, 2001.

————. *Tarot Shadow Work*. St. Paul, Minn.: Llewellyn Publications, 2000.

Hitchcock, Helyn. *Helping Yourself with Numerology*. West Nyack, N.Y.: Parker Publishing Company, Inc., 1972.

Kunz, George Frederick. *The Curious Lore of Precious Stones*. Copyright 1913 by J. B. Lippincott Company, Philadelphia, Pa.; copyright renewed 1941 by Ruby Kunz Zinsser; published 1971 by Dover Publications, Inc., New York, N.Y., by special arrangement with J. P. Lippincott Company.

Lewis, Anthony. *Tarot Plain and Simple*. St. Paul, Minn.: Llewellyn Publications, 1966.

Melody. *Love is in the Earth: A Kaleidoscope of Crystals*. Wheat Ridge, Colo.: Earth-Love Publishing House, 1995.

Morrison, Dorothy. *Everyday Magic*. St. Paul, Minn.: Llewellyn Publications, 1998.

————. *The Whimsical Tarot: A Deck for Children and the Young at Heart*. Stamford, Conn.: U.S. Games Systems, Inc., 2001.

Renée, Janina. *Tarot Spells*. St. Paul, Minn.: Llewellyn Publications, 1990.

————. *Tarot: Your Everyday Guide.* St. Paul, Minn.: Llewellyn Publications, 2000.

Riva, Anna. *The Modern Herbal Spellbook: The Magical Uses of Herbs.* Toluca Lake, Calif.: International Imports, 1974.

Sterling, Stephen Walter. *Tarot Awareness.* St. Paul, Minn.: Llewellyn Publications, 2000.

Index

REACH FOR THE MOON

Llewellyn publishes hundreds of books on your favorite subjects! To get these exciting books, including the ones on the following pages, check your local bookstore or order them directly from Llewellyn.

Order by Phone

- Call toll-free within the U.S. and Canada, 1-877-NEW-WRLD
- In Minnesota, call (651) 291-1970
- We accept VISA, MasterCard, and American Express

Order by Mail

- Send the full price of your order (MN residents add 7% sales tax) in U.S. funds, plus postage & handling to:
  Llewellyn Worldwide
  P.O. Box 64383, Dept. (0-7387-0175-0)
  St. Paul, MN 55164–0383, U.S.A.

Postage & Handling

- Standard (U.S., Mexico, & Canada)
  If your order is:
  $20 or under, add $5
  $20.01–$100, add $6
  Over $100, shipping is free

(Continental U.S. orders ship UPS. AK, HI, PR, & P.O. Boxes ship USPS 1st class. Mex. & Can. ship PMB.)

- Second Day Air (Continental U.S. only): $10 for one book plus $1 per each additional book
- Express (AK, HI, & PR only) [Not available for P.O. Box delivery. For street address delivery only.]: $15 for one book plus $1 per each additional book
- International Surface Mail: $20 or under, add $5 plus $1 per item; $20.01 and over, add $6 plus $1 per item
- International Airmail: Books—Add the retail price of each item Non-book items—Add $5 per item

Please allow 4–6 weeks for delivery on all orders.
Postage and handling rates subject to change.

Discounts

We offer a 20% discount to group leaders or agents. You must order a minimum of 5 copies of the same book to get our special quantity price.

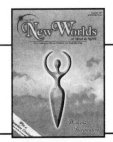

FREE CATALOG
Get a free copy of our color catalog, New Worlds of Mind and Spirit. Subscribe for just $10.00 in the United States and Canada ($30.00 overseas, airmail). Call 1-877-NEW-WRLD today!

Visit our website at www.llewellyn.com for more information.

Everyday Magic

Spells & Rituals for Modern Living

Dorothy Morrison

Are you tired of looking for ritual solutions for today's problems: computer viruses, traffic that drives you crazy, and stress that makes you forget your own name? Does the quest for obscure spell ingredients leave you exhausted and empty-handed?

Now there's a better way to incorporate magic into your life without adding more stress to it. *Everyday Magic* updates the ancient arts to fit today's lifestyle. It promotes the use of modern convenience items as viable magical tools, and it incorporates the use of easy-to-find spell ingredients—most of which are already in your kitchen cabinet.

More than 300 spells and rituals cover the everyday concerns of the modern practitioner.

- Set your spell into motion and speed up the results with "magical boosters"
- Magnify your focused intent and energy flow with herbs, flowers, trees, and stones
- Learn how to perform ancient arts with modern tools: your coffee maker, blender, and crock pot
- Make your own magical powders, sachets, bath salts, potpourris, incenses, and oils
- Practice spells for more than 300 purposes

1-56718-469-3, 304 pp., 5⅜ x 8   **$9.95**

To order, call 1-877-NEW-WRLD

Prices subject to change without notice

Tarot: Your Everyday Guide

Practical Problem Solving and
Everyday Advice

Janina Renée

Whenever people begin to read the tarot, they inevitably find
themselves asking the cards, "What should I do about such-
and-such situation?" Yet there is little information available
on how to get those answers from the cards.

Reading the tarot for advice requires a different approach
than reading for prediction, so the card descriptions in *Tarot:
Your Everyday Guide* are adapted accordingly. You interpret a
card in terms of things that you can do, and the central figure in the card, which usually represents the querent, models
what ought to be done.

This book is especially concerned with practical matters,
applying the tarot's advice to common problems and situations that many people are concerned about, such as whether
to say "yes" or "no" to an offer, whether or not to become
involved in some cause or conflict, choosing between job and
educational options, starting or ending relationships, and
dealing with difficult people.

1-56718-565-7, 312 pp., 7½ x 9⅛   **$12.95**

To order, call 1-877-NEW-WRLD

Prices subject to change without notice

The Sacred Circle Tarot

A Celtic Pagan Journey

Anna Franklin
illustrated by Paul Mason

The Sacred Circle Tarot is a new concept in tarot design, combining photographs, computer imaging, and traditional drawing techniques to create stunning images. It draws on the Pagan heritage of Britain and Ireland, its sacred sites and landscapes. Key symbols unlock the deepest levels of Pagan teaching.

The imagery of the cards is designed to work on a number of levels, serving as a tool not only for divination but to facilitate meditation, personal growth, and spiritual development. The "sacred circle" refers to the progress of the initiate from undirected energy, through dawning consciousness, to the death of the old self and the emergence of the new.

The major arcana is modified somewhat to fit the pagan theme of the deck. For example, "The Fool" becomes "The Green Man," "The Hierophant" becomes "The Druid," and "The World" becomes "The World Tree." The accompanying book gives a full explanation of the symbolism in the cards and their divinatory meanings.

1-56718-457-X, Boxed Kit, 78 full-color cards,
288 pp. book, 6 x 9   **$29.95**

To order, call 1-877-NEW-WRLD

Prices subject to change without notice

The Nigel Jackson Tarot

Nigel Jackson

This breathtaking new tarot deck by world-renowned artist Nigel Jackson is both a return to authentic medieval-renaissance symbolism and an amazing breakthrough in our knowledge of the authentic nature and meaning of the Tarot images.

For three centuries, scholars have speculated on the origins of the Tarot. Now Nigel Jackson presents his original theory concerning the medievalized Orphic-Pythagorean numerology underpinning of the cards, which could revolutionize our understanding of the Tarot and the secret tradition on which it lies.

The Neo-Pythagorean magical origin advanced by *The Nigel Jackson Tarot* is perhaps the first serious attempt in this century to reassess the Tarot tradition in a fresh and insightful way. It places this enigmatic oracle in its true context, that of late Graeco-Roman mystery-wisdom.

1-56718-365-4, Boxed Mini-Kit, 78 cards
160 pp. mini-book in slip case   **$24.95**

To order, call 1-877-NEW-WRLD

Prices subject to change without notice